# ITALIAN
# VEGETARIAN
# COOKING

# ITALIAN VEGETARIAN COOKING

*Paola Gavin*

*M. EVANS AND COMPANY*
*NEW YORK*

M. Evans and Company, Inc.
216 East 49 Street
New York, New York 10017


**Library of Congress Cataloging-in-Publication Data**

Gavin, Paola.
    Italian vegetarian cooking / Paola Gavin. — New, rev. ed.
      p.  cm.
    Includes index.
    ISBN 0-87131-769-9 (pbk.) : $12.95
    1. Vegetarian cookery. 2. Cookery, Italian. I. Title.
TX837.G34   1994
641.5′636′0945—dc20                    94-30639
                                            CIP


Design by Manuela Paul

Manufactured in the United States of America

9  8  7  6  5  4  3  2  1

*To Francesca,*
*Bianca, and Seana*

# CONTENTS

# INTRODUCTION

The cooking of Italy has been closely related to a vegetarian diet for many centuries. In ancient Rome, peasants lived on a basic diet of broth, pasta, vegetables, beans, and fruit. In the Renaissance, when Italy looked to ancient Greece and Rome for a rebirth of art and ideas, there was a new interest in vegetarianism, perhaps because Pythagoras and Hippocrates, the founders of modern medicine, were both vegetarians. Leonardo da Vinci, the greatest artist and thinker of his times, was a vegetarian.

Today, Italy is divided into nineteen regions, each of which has its own unique cultural heritage. Over the centuries parts of Italy have been ruled by Etruscans, Romans, Greeks, Saracens, Lombards, Normans, Spaniards, Austrians, and many others. Each of these cultures has left its mark on the cuisine of these regions, making Italian cooking one of the most varied and exciting in Europe.

Gastronomically, Italy divides into two main areas. This division is, in part, due to simple economics. The more prosperous North uses butter, or a combination of butter and olive oil, as the main cooking fat. Pasta is generally made with eggs. Cattle graze on the rich pastures, especially in Lombardy, making cheese and dairy products plentiful. The South, much of which is poverty stricken, uses olive oil almost exclusively as the main cooking fat. Olive trees grow well on the dry, arid soil and are less expensive to maintain than cattle. Pasta is generally factory made, without eggs. Meat is a luxury, generally eaten once a week on Sundays. Vegetables are cheap and the growing season is virtually all year round. So the diet of the South naturally leans toward a vegetarian diet just as it did in the days of ancient Rome.

The recipes in this book have been collected over the years

while I was living in Rome and traveling through the regions of Italy. Some recipes were given to me by dear Italian friends, some I adapted from old Italian cookbooks, many I discovered while traveling and eating in the local *trattorie,* where much of the best regional cooking is to be found.

Most of the recipes are simple to prepare. Italian regional cooking is, after all, a peasant cuisine, a *cucina casalinga* (homestyle cooking), which leaves plenty of room for the individual touch (or error)! As Waverley Root writes in his book *The Food of Italy,* ". . . while French cooking has become professional cooking even when it is executed by amateurs, Italian cooking has remained basically amateur cooking even when it is executed by professionals."

All of these influences add up to a simple, healthful cuisine, based on natural ingredients, using the freshest of produce, always in season, making Italy, of all the countries I have ever visited, a veritable vegetarian paradise.

—P.G.

# REGIONS AND THEIR SPECIALTIES

### Piedmont and the Valla d'Aosta

Piedmont and the Valle d'Aosta lie in the northwest corner of Italy, backing up against the French and Swiss Alps. The cooking of Piedmont is strongly influenced by the cooking of France. (Piedmont was once part of French Savoy.) Piedmont's most famous dish, *fonduta*, is reminiscent of the French and Swiss fondues.

The most prized food of Piedmont is the white truffle, found in the hills around Mondovi and the region of Alba. This truffle is usually sliced paper-thin and added sparingly to enhance the flavor of a dish.

Turin, the elegant capital of Piedmont, is the home of *grissini*, thin bread sticks that are claimed to be the most easily digested form of bread.

Piedmont produces some of the most famous cheeses in Italy; Robbiole, Toma and Tomini, and, of course, Fontina. Butter and cream are used everywhere for cooking.

This is polenta and rice country. The Po Valley, which runs through Piedmont, Lombardy, and the Veneto, is Italy's main rice-producing region.

The Piedmontese make excellent desserts, especially custards and creams. They are very fond of chocolate. In fact, desserts *alla piemontese* usually mean "with chocolate."

Piedmont produces some of the finest wines in Italy: Barolo, Barbera, Freisa, Grignolino, Dolcetto, Barberesco, Gattinara (which is especially good with rice and truffle dishes), and Nebbiolo. The most famous white wine is the sparkling dessert wine, Asti Spumante. Piedmont is also the major producer of the apéritif Vermouth, which is made from white wine, herbs, and spices.

## LOCAL SPECIALTIES

*INSALATA DI FONTINA:* Fontina cheese salad with green olives and sweet peppers, in a mustard cream dressing.

*INSALATA DI RISO ALLA PIEMONTESE:* Rice salad with asparagus tips, celery, *ovoli* mushrooms, and truffle.

*FONDUTA:* Cheese fondue made with eggs, milk, fontina cheese, and truffle.

*CARCIOFI ALLO ZABAGLIONE:* Artichokes served with an egg and wine sauce.

*POLENTA PASTICCIATA CON FUNGHI:* A layered pie of polenta, mushrooms, fontina cheese, béchamel sauce, and grated cheese.

*POLENTA IN CAROZZA:* Fried polenta sandwiches filled with fontina cheese.

*RISO IN CAGNON:* Rice with melted fontina cheese.

*RISOTTO AL BARBERA:* Rice with barbera wine.

*CISRÀ:* Chick-pea and turnip soup.

*TURTA:* A rice and spinach pie.

*POMODORO RIPIENE ALLA NOVARESE:* Tomatoes stuffed with rice, onions, and herbs.

*PATATE TARTUFATE:* A potato casserole with cheese and truffles.

*BONET:* A chocolate-almond baked custard.

*PESCHE RIPIENE:* Peaches stuffed with sugar, wine, and crushed macaroons, and topped with whipped cream.

*CILIEGIE IN BAROLO:* Cherries cooked in Barolo wine with orange rind and cinnamon.

## Lombardy

Lombardy is a region of contrasts. It is both the garden of Italy and the most industrialized region in the country, with Milan its cosmopolitan center of business. The cooking of Lombardy is so diverse that many of its ancient cities, such as Bergamo, Pavia, Brescia, Como, Cremona, and Mantua, claim their own cuisines.

The landscape is equally varied, with great alpine slopes in the north covered with dense forests and fine mountain pastures, and the breathtaking Italian lakes, which give way to the rich agricultural plain in the south and the Po Valley.

Rice is the most important crop in the Po Valley. The Milanese eat more rice than they do pasta. Corn is grown as well as other superb vegetables and fruits. Honey, walnuts, chestnuts, and wine grapes are all cultivated in the hills to the north. Butter rather than olive oil is the main cooking fat.

Saffron, imported from the Abruzzi region, is a favorite flavoring in Milan. In the Middle Ages, alchemists used gold to color food, as they believed it cured many ills. Saffron continues this tradition, as it also colors food yellow and is purported to have medicinal qualities.

Tomatoes are used sparingly. When they are incorporated in a dish, only enough is added to give a rose color.

Lombardy produces some of the best cheeses in Italy: Gorgonzola, Bel Paese, the delicate cream cheese—Mascarpone, Grana or Parmesan-type cheese from Lodi, and the Italian version of Gruyère cheese, Groviera.

The cooking of Milan is much influenced by Austrian cooking (Lombardy was once part of the Austrian empire). This is especially noticeable in the love of rich pastries and whipped cream *(lattemiele)*. There is also a strong French influence, which carries over into the language. Milanese dialect uses the French word *tomate* rather than the Italian *pomodoro*, and *artichaut* for artichoke rather than the Italian *carciofo*.

The best wines of Lombardy come from the Valtellina Valley—Sassella, Grumello, and Inferno. The famous, slightly bitter apéritif Campari, is made in Milan.

## LOCAL SPECIALTIES

*ASPARAGII ALLA LOMBARDA:* Boiled asparagus served with butter and grated cheese, topped with fried eggs.

*POLENTA TARAGNA:* Buckwheat polenta with fresh cheese *(fiore di latte)*.

*POLENTA PASTICCIATA:* Polenta layered with béchamel sauce, mushrooms, and Gruyère cheese and baked in the oven.

*PIZZOCHERI:* Buckwheat noodles cooked with potatoes, green beans, cabbage, and grated cheese, quickly baked in the oven.

*RIS E SPARGITT:* Rice with asparagus.

*RISOTTO ALLA MILANESE:* Rice cooked in broth or white wine, saffron, butter, and pepper; sometimes topped with sautéed dried mushrooms or truffles.

*LA RISOTTA:* A very creamy risotto made with onions and saffron.

*TORTELLI ALLA CREMASCA:* Ravioli stuffed with crushed macaroons, grated cheese, brandy, nutmeg, and egg yolks, served with melted butter and grated cheese.

*TORTELLI DI ZUCCA:* Ravioli stuffed with pumpkin, eggs, crushed macaroons, Verona mustard (more a chutney than a mustard), and candied citron, served with sage butter and grated cheese.

*SCARPAZZA:* A spinach or cabbage tart.

*MINESTRONE ALLA MILANESE:* A very thick vegetable soup, thickened with rice, never pasta. May be served cold in the summer.

*ZUPPA PAVESE:* A soup of broth, eggs, fried bread, and grated cheese. A specialty of Pavia.

*BROCCOLI ALLA MILANESE:* Boiled broccoli, dipped into cheese-flavored eggs, then into bread crumbs, and fried in butter.

*MOZZARELLA MILANESE:* A misnomer; Bell Paese is always used. The cheese is dipped into flour, then egg, then bread crumbs, and deep-fried.

*TORTA DEL PARADISO:* A very light and delicate cake, flavored with vanilla and lemon rind.

*PANETTONE:* The traditional Italian Christmas cake; a simple cake, similar to a brioche, with raisins, candied peel, and citron.

*CREMA DI MASCARPONE:* Mascarpone cream cheese mixed with rum, sugar, egg yolks, and cinnamon.

*TORRONE:* Nougat made with honey, almonds, egg white, and candied peel. A specialty of Cremona.

## Trentino and Alto Adige

The Alto Adige belonged to Austria until World War I, when, under the Treaty of Versailles, it was given to Italy. The landscape is spectacular. Here lies the majestic Marmolada mountain, the highest in the Dolomites. The valleys spilling into the Adige River are very fertile; rye, wheat, corn, oats, and barley are cultivated. Vines and fruit trees are grown on the hillsides. This is the only region of Italy that cultivates raspberries.

The vegetables grown are simple and Teutonic in character: red and white cabbages, potatoes, turnips, and kohlrabi. The *trattorie* serve German-sounding dishes. *Knödeln* and *Canederli* for *gnocchi*, *Schwammerlsuppe* is a cream of mushroom soup; *Riebl* is a fritter made of buckwheat flour.

The local breads are often heavy and made of mixed grains, like the bread of Merano and the barley bread, Brazadel. They are often flavored with caraway seeds, believed to be an aphrodisiac.

There is a fondness for pastries and sweets that reflects the Austro-Hungarian background. Excellent strudels are made, filled with apples, pears, cherries, or sour cream *(Rahmstrudel)*; also, fruit-filled pancakes *(Schmarren)* and fritters *(frittelle)*.

The wines of the region are excellent. The most noted white wines are Termeno, which is particularly good with antipasti and egg. Riesling and Terlano are excellent with minestrone and bean soups. Santa Maddalena, Teroldego, and Lagreinkretzer are also superior red wines.

## LOCAL SPECIALTIES

**ZUPPA DI FARINA ABBRUSTOLITA:** A potato and milk soup thickened with flour.

**SCHWAMMERLSUPPE:** Cream of mushroom soup.

**ZWIEBELSUPPE:** A gruel-like onion soup flavored with sugar and vinegar.

**MUS:** A cornmeal and wheat milk soup, with the consistency of porridge.

**GNOCCHI TIROLESI NERI:** Buckwheat and rye flour gnocchi.

**TÜRTELN:** Rye-flour ravioli, stuffed with cabbage

or sauerkraut, flavored with onion, caraway seeds, chives, and marjoram.

**FRITTATA ALLA TRENTINA:** A fluffy omelet. May be served with tomato, mushroom or cheese filling.

**ERDBEERTORTE:** Raspberry tart.

**PRESNITZ:** A pastry with an elaborate filling of almonds, walnuts, bread crumbs, butter, sugar, white raisins, chocolate, lemon rind, citron, rum, and vanilla.

**KRAPFEN:** Doughnuts.

**PANE TIROLESI:** A light sweet bread flavored with almonds, lemon, and cinnamon.

## Veneto

The cooking of the Veneto, or Venezia Euganea, is one of the most elegant in Italy. The city of Venice, with its ornate palaces lining the famous Grand Canal, is a constant reminder that it was the most affluent city in Europe in the Middle Ages. Its wealth came from the spice trade with Constantinople and the Orient. It was to Venice that sugar, pepper, nutmeg, cloves, ginger, and coffee were first brought, and then distributed around Europe.

The Veneto Region includes the ancient cities of Vicenza, Padua, Treviso, and Verona (immortalized by Romeo and Juliet), the eastern shore of Lake Garda, and a portion of the Dolomite Alps in the north with the famous ski resort of Cortina d'Ampezzo.

Artichokes, peas, cabbages, zucchini, pumpkin, onions, tomatoes, and the famous asparagus of Bassano are cultivated in the southerly plains. Mushrooms, peaches, and grape vines are grown in the hills. Rice, grown in the Po Valley, is eaten more than pasta in the Veneto. Rice is served with an enormous variety of vegetables. The most famous rice dish is *risi e bisi*, rice with peas, using the tiniest, most tender, sweetest peas found in May and June.

The town of Treviso, with its canals and delightful market, is famous for *radicchio rosso*, or red chicory, which is grown nowhere else in Italy.

The best beans in Italy are from Lamon, in Belluno province where, of course, bean soups are enjoyed.

The Veneto is celebrated for its cakes and pastries, many of which include cornmeal. Three cheeses are produced in the region: Asiago, made near Vicenza; Ricotta; and Casatella, a soft, buttery cheese made from cow's milk.

The wines of the Veneto are superior. The best known are Soave, Valpolicella, Bardolino, Garganega, Prosecco, and Tokai. Tokai, Soave, and Valpolicella are all especially good with pasta.

## LOCAL SPECIALTIES

**RISI E BISI:** Rice and peas.

**RISI E FASOI:** Rice and beans.

**RISI E CAVOLI:** Rice, cauliflower, onion, garlic, butter, oil, and sage.

**RISI E ZUCCA:** Rice and pumpkin cooked in butter and milk.

**RISI E PORRI:** Rice with leeks.

**RISO CO' LA UA:** Rice with Málaga grapes and, sometimes, pine nuts.

**RISI CON FENOCI:** Rice with fennel.

**BIGOLI CON LE NOCI:** Whole wheat noodles with walnut sauce.

**GNOCCHI PADOVANI:** Potato gnocchi, made with buckwheat flour.

**GNOCCHI ALLA VERONESE:** Potato gnocchi served with sugar, cinnamon, and grated cheese.

**POLENTA FASOLA:** Polenta with beans.

**COLOMBA DI PASQUA:** An Easter cake flavored

with cloves, cinnamon, almonds, kirsch, and orange rind.

**PANDORO VERONESE:** A dome-shaped cake flavored with rum and vanilla.

**TORTA SAVIOSA:** A cake made with cornmeal, potato flour, butter, vanilla, sugar, eggs, and aniseed.

**TORTA DI ZUCCA:** Pumpkin cake.

**COTINFE:** A simple dessert made of dried apples cooked in wine and sweetened with honey.

## Friuli and Venezia Giulia

Friuli and Venezia Giulia lie in the Northeast of Italy, bordering on Yugoslavia and Austria. The region is largely mountainous and not very fertile. Corn, root vegetables, artichokes, and asparagus are grown in the Friuli plain.

This is the poorest region in northern Italy. Bread and vegetables are the mainstay of the diet. Vegetable *frittate* (omelets) are popular, with strange dialect names. *Fertae cu lis jerbúzzis* is a mixed herb omelet that includes nasturtium leaves.

Many of the rice dishes of the Veneto are found here. Montasio cheese, somewhat similar to Emmentaler cheese, is made in the province of Udine.

This is wine country. Some of the names are confusing, as they are the same as many of the wines from the Trentino and Alto Adige. Tocai, Riesling, Traminer, Sauvignon, and Pinot Blanc are fine white wines. Merlot, Cabernet Franc, and Pinot Nero are the best known red wines.

## LOCAL SPECIALTIES

**FRICCO:** Fresh cheese and apples cooked with butter, served as an antipasto.

**MINESTRA DI RISO ALLA FRIULIANA:** Rice soup with egg, lemon, and grated cheese.

*IOTA:* Bean and sauerkraut soup.

*PAPAROT:* A thick soup of cornmeal and spinach.

*SOPA FRIULIANA:* Celery soup, traditionally served on Christmas Eve.

*CIARSCONS ALLA CARNIOLA:* Ravioli stuffed with ricotta cheese, raisins, parsley, bread crumbs, and spices.

*FERTAE CUI CESARONS:* Frittata made with onion, leek, peas, and fennel.

*FRITOLE DI FENOCI:* Fennel fritters.

*ZASTOCH:* Green bean, potato, and pumpkin stew.

*BROVADA:* Marinated turnips, fried in olive oil and garlic and flavored with caraway seeds.

## Liguria

Liguria is the narrow coastal region hugging the Gulf of Genoa in the Northwest. It stretches from the French border in the West to La Spezia and the border of Tuscany in the East. It is largely mountainous, with a spectacular coast road that tunnels through terraced hillsides that drop precipitously down to the blue sea below. This is the Italian Rivieria, with such famous resort towns as San Remo, Portofino, and Santa Margherita.

The main city is Genoa, which rivals Bologna as the gastronomic capital of Italy. Genoa is famous for its green basil sauce, *pesto,* which is lavished on pasta, and used in soups and ravioli.

The whole region abounds with fresh fruits and vegetables, especially green vegetables and herbs of all kinds: marjoram, oregano, parsley, bay leaf, sage, fennel, rosemary. Walnuts, pine nuts, olives, and capers are all used profusely.

The cuisine of Liguria excels in its vegetable cookery. Vegetable tarts, gratins, and stuffed vegetables of all kinds are made.

Very little cheese is made in Liguria except ricotta, which is made in Savona. The most common cheese used is Pecorino Sardo, imported from Sardinia.

The Ligurians, like their French neighbors, are fond of sweet pastries and candied fruits, especially *marrons glacés* (candied chestnuts).

Liguria produces few wines. The most notable is the dry rosé Dolceaqua and the white wine from the villages of the Cinque Terre, near La Spezia.

## LOCAL SPECIALTIES

*PESTO ALLA GENOVESE:* A sauce of fresh basil, olive oil, pecorino sardo cheese, and pine nuts.

*CONDIJON:* A mixed salad with onion, sweet pepper, tomato, olives, and capers.

*SARDENAIRA:* A pizza topped with black olives, capers, garlic, and marjoram.

*LA TORTA PASQUALINA:* Literally, "Easter Tart"—a specialty of Genoa. Paper-thin sheets of pastry filled with spinach, ricotta cheese, eggs, and herbs. Artichokes are sometimes substituted for spinach.

*LA TORTA DI FUNGHI E ZUCCHINI:* Similar to La Torta Pasqualina, but with a filling of mushrooms, zucchini, ricotta cheese, eggs, and herbs.

*TRENETTE COL PESTO:* Ribbon noodles cooked with potatoes and tiny green beans.

*MINESTRONE ALLA GENOVESE:* A thick vegetable soup flavored with pesto sauce.

*PREBOGGION:* Rice and herb soup flavored with pesto sauce.

*FRITTATA DI BIETOLE:* Swiss chard omelet with onion, grated cheese, and oregano.

*TAGGIAEN VERDI:* Green tagliarini noodles

made with Swiss chard, spinach, and borage, served with mushroom sauce and grated cheese.

*TROFFIE ALLA GENOVESE:* Potato gnocchi served with butter, pesto sauce, and grated cheese.

*POLPETTONE DI FAGIOLINI:* A green bean and potato pie.

*FOCACCIA ALLA SALVIA:* Sage bread.

*PAN DOLCE:* "Sweet bread" with white raisins, pine nuts, and candied fruit. A specialty of Genoa.

## Tuscany

Tuscany is one of the largest regions of Italy. Although not quite the geographic center, to many Italians it is the heart of Italy. Certainly it was the heart of the Renaissance.

It is hard not to talk in superlatives when speaking of Tuscany. It has produced some of the greatest artists, writers, and thinkers of all time: Michelangelo, Leonardo da Vinci, Piero della Francesca, Botticelli, Fra' Angelico, Giotto, Boccaccio, and Galileo, to name just a few. Some of the most beautiful towns in Italy are found here: Florence, Siena, Lucca, Arezzo, San Gimignano, and Pisa.

Tuscan speech is Italian in its purest form. The countryside, mainly gently rolling hills covered with olive groves, vineyards, and pastures, is both peaceful and inspiring. It has a long coastline of white sandy beaches. Many a passing traveler has fallen under its spell and stayed a lifetime.

The Tuscans have a distaste for excess, inherited perhaps from their Etruscan ancestors. Tuscans are simple and refined and so is their cooking, which relies upon the combination of the finest ingredients and the artistry of their cooks. Few sauces and garnishes disguise the natural flavor of the food. They are masters of vegetable cookery, especially of the haricot bean, brought from

America in the sixteenth century. Tuscans are so fond of beans that a Tuscan is often referred to in other parts of the country as a *mangiafagioli* or "bean-eater." They rival the Romans in the cooking of artichokes. The best olive oil is purported to come from Lucca, although most Tuscans use luscious green olive oil from olives grown and pressed in their local villages. Butter is often combined with olive oil in cooking.

The most famous wine of Tuscany is Chianti, of which there are many grades. Chianti Classico is always of top quality. Brunello di Montalcino is another fine red wine, as is Carmignano and the sweet dessert wine from Elba, Aleatico di Portferraio.

## LOCAL SPECIALTIES

*ACQUACOTTA:* "Cooked water," a vegetable broth with onions, celery, and tomatoes, poured over eggs, cheese, and bread.

*LA CIPOLLATA:* An onion soup.

*L'INFARINATA:* A vegetable soup thickened with cornmeal.

*ZUPPA DI FAGIOLI:* A thick bean soup served over toast.

*LA RIBOLLITA: Zuppa di fagioli,* cooled and reheated (reboiled) with more olive oil and gratinéed in the oven.

*LA FETTE:* A black cabbage *(cavolo neri)* soup.

*STROZZAPRETI ALLA FIORENTINA:* Spinach and ricotta gnocchi.

*STRICCHE E CECI:* Noodles and chick-peas, flavored with garlic, olive oil, and rosemary.

*RISOTTO ALLA TOSCANA:* A summer risotto with tomato, zucchini, peas, and asparagus tips.

*ASPARAGI ALLA FIORENTINA:* Boiled asparagus sautéed in butter, topped with grated cheese and fried eggs.

*TORTINO DI CARCIOFI:* A baked artichoke omelet.

*FAGIOLI AL FIASCO:* Dried white beans cooked in a wine flask with olive oil, garlic, and sage.

*FAGIOLI ALL'UCCELLETTO:* Boiled dried white beans, cooked with olive oil, garlic, sage, and tomato purée.

*CASTAGNACCIO:* A pizza or flat cake made of chestnut flour, topped with raisins, pine nuts, and fennel seeds.

*CENCI ALLA FIORENTINA:* Ribbons of dough, tied in bowties, fried in oil and dusted with sugar.

*PANFORTE DI SIENA:* A rich fruitcake made with almonds, walnuts, candied watermelon, orange rind, sugar, flour, and spices.

*RICCIARELLI DI SIENA:* Almond macaroons.


## Emilia-Romagna

Emilia-Romagna is bounded by the Po River in the North, the Adriatic Sea in the East, and the Apennine Mountains in the South and West. It consists mainly of a rich, fertile plain, dotted with some of the most ancient towns in Italy—Piacenza, Parma, Bologna, Ferrara, Modena, and Ravenna.

Bologna, city of medieval arcades and towers (two of which seem to lean over as much as the famous leaning Tower of Pisa), is nicknamed *La Grassa* or "fat one," due to its rich and fattening cuisine. Many Italians consider Bologna the gastronomic capital of Italy.

Fruits and vegetables are grown in abundance, especially table grapes, apples, pears, peaches, strawberries, tomatoes, sugar beets, asparagus, potatoes, zucchini, and almonds. Wheat is also cultivated. Emilia-Romagna is famous for its pasta. Lasagna is said to have been invented here.

Butter and olive oil are both used in cooking. The creamy butter of the region *(burro di panna)*, is much sought after in the rest of Italy.

Perhaps the most famous product of Emilia-Romagna is Parmesan cheese, or Parmigiano-Reggiano, as it is called in Italy. The cheese is made in the areas of Parma, Reggio nell'Emilia, and Modena. All other Parmesan cheese made outside this controlled area is called *grana*.

Lambrusco is the best known wine of Emilia-Romagna, but it does not travel well. Sangiovese and Vino Rosso del Bosco are two wines worthy of note. Several good liqueurs are distilled here, including Nocino (made from walnuts), Sassolino (made from star anise imported from China), Rosolio and various fruit-flavored brandies.

## LOCAL SPECIALTIES

*PASSATELLI IN BRODO:* Spinach dumplings in broth.

*TORTELLE D'ERBETTE:* Ring-shaped ravioli stuffed with spinach and herbs.

*CAPPELLACCI CON LA ZUCCA:* Ravioli with pumpkin stuffing. A specialty of Ferrara.

*TORTEI CON LA CUA:* Butterfly-shaped ravioli stuffed with ricotta cheese and herbs.

*TAGLIATELLE ALLA SALSA DI NOCI:* Noodles with ricotta cheese, butter, grated cheese, and crushed walnuts.

*RAVIOLI CON FORMAGGIO:* Ravioli stuffed with cottage cheese, cinnamon, nutmeg, cloves, and saffron. A specialty of Faenza.

*ASPARAGI ALLA PARMIGIANA:* Boiled asparagus topped with butter and grated cheese, baked in the oven.

***CARCIOFI ALLA PARMIGIANA:*** Boiled artichoke hearts in cream sauce topped with grated cheese and baked in the oven.

***ERBAZZONE DOLCE:*** A sweet Swiss chard pie with ricotta cheese, sugar, almonds, rum, and lemon rind.

***PAMPETATO DI CIOCCOLATO:*** A chocolate cake made with honey, milk, almonds, lemon rind, pepper, and spices.

***FRITTATE DOLCE DI PIGNOLI:*** Sweet pine-nut fritters, flambéed in rum.

***AMARETTI:*** Macaroons.

***LA BONISSIMA:*** A light cake flavored with vanilla and lemon, with a filling of honey, rum, crushed walnuts, and chocolate.

## Umbria

Like Lombardy, Umbria is the only region in Italy that has no coastline. It has several lakes, the largest being Lake Trasimeno. The landscape, with its rolling hills and ancient hill towns, is that of medieval paintings come to life. Here is Assisi, birthplace of St. Francis, Gubbio, Spoleto, and Perugia—a delightful citadel, perched on a mountain ridge surrounded by Roman walls and Etruscan ramparts.

The valleys are often steep but fertile, with sheep and goats grazing in the hills. In the lowlands wheat, vegetables, olives, and fruits are grown. Plums and figs are dried for export. Many varieties of mushrooms are grown. The best known are the black truffles of Norcia and Spoleto. The Romans believed them to be an aphrodisiac. There is an old saying that goes: "Those who wish to lead virtuous lives should abstain from eating truffles."

Perugia has a sweet tooth. The streets and alleys are filled with pastry shops. The famous Perugina chocolates are made here.

Umbria is not known for its cheeses, but two cheeses are produced: Caciotto, made from cow's milk, and Pecorino.

Orvieto is unrivaled as the best wine of Umbria. Dry, white, and pleasing it has been a favorite of cardinals and painters for centuries. Orvieto also makes a fine Vino Santo.

## LOCAL SPECIALTIES

*CIPOLLATA:* Onion soup with tomato, thickened with egg.

*SPAGHETTI AD AGLIO ED OLIO:* Spaghetti with garlic, olive oil, and hot pepper.

*CIRIOLE TERNANA:* Long hollow noodles, dressed with olive oil, garlic and tomato and mushroom sauce.

*SPAGHETTI ALLA NOCI:* Spaghetti with a sauce of walnuts, pine nuts, and garlic.

*STRANGOZZI DI SPOLETO:* Ribbon noodles with tomato sauce, herbs, and garlic.

*FRITTATA DI TARTUFI:* Truffle omelet.

*SEDANI DI TREVI IN UMIDO:* Fresh celery in tomato sauce.

*TORTA COL FORMAGGIO:* Cheesecake.

*CICERCHIATA:* "Chick-peas" or nuts of dough, deep-fried, coated with boiling honey and left to set.

*PESTRINGOLO:* A very rich fruitcake made of dried figs, raisins, almonds, pine nuts, candied peel, bread crumbs, cocoa, honey, and spices.

*PINOCCHIATE:* Candied pine nuts, flavored with orange and lemon rind.

## Le Marche

The Marches, or Le Marche as it is called by the Italians, is a lesser known region of Italy. It consists of rolling hills descending from the Apennine ridge of mountains in the West, to the Adriatic Sea in the east. The coastline is dotted with a handful of fishing villages and several small resort towns, including Pesaro and Senigallia, more popular with Italian tourists than with the more sophisticated foreigner; Ancona, the capital of the Marches, is the main seaport of the central Adriatic. Unfortunately, much of the old town was destroyed in the two World Wars.

The Marches is largely agricultural. Vegetables, fruit trees, olives, wine grapes, and wheat are grown. Sheep and goats graze on the hillsides.

The most outstanding town in the region is the graceful hill town of Urbino, with its fine Ducal palace built by one of the greatest patrons of the Renaissance, Federigo da Montrefeltro.

The only well-known wine of the region is the bright straw colored Verdicchio dei Castelli di Jesi. Vino Santo is made in Urbino.

## LOCAL SPECIALTIES

*PISSELATA ALLA MACERATESE:* Pea soup with onion, tomato, garlic, and herbs.

*ZUPPA DI FAGIOLI ALL'ANCONETANA:* Bean soup cooked with garlic, celery, parsley, and *peperoncini.*

*CROCCHETTE DI UOVA ALLA MARCHIGIANA:* Egg croquettes.

*CALCIONI (RAVIOLI ALL'ASCOLANA):* Ravioli stuffed with fresh pecorino cheese, egg yolks, sugar, lemon, and grated cheese, topped with grated cheese and oil and baked in the oven.

*RISOTTO ALLA ROSSINI:* Rice with egg and mushrooms.

*PIZZA AL FORMAGGIO:* Cheese bread made with Parmesan, pecorino and Gruyere cheeses.

*FAVE ALLA CAMPAGNOLA:* Fava beans served with onion sauce.

*FRITTATA CO' LA MINDUCCIA:* Omelet flavored with mint.

*CIAMBELLE COL MOSTO:* Ring-shaped cake flavored with wine.

*BOSTRENGO:* A chocolate rice pudding flavored with rum, cinnamon, and maraschino.

## Rome and the Lazio

Rome dominates the cooking of the Lazio. It combines the cooking of the North with cooking of the South. It is a simple but robust cuisine, not unlike the cooking of Tuscany.

The streets of Rome abound with restaurants and *trattorie,* especially in the charming Trastevere quarter. Eating out in Rome is a way of life. It has earned its nickname "City of a Thousand Meals."

The Lazio is wine and olive country. Vegetables, especially broccoli, peas, fennel, artichokes, and tomatoes, grow well in the countryside around Rome, as can be seen by the abundant produce at the famous Campo dei Fiori market in Old Rome.

Mint is a characteristic flavor of Roman cooking. Vegetables are often dressed simply with garlic, olive oil, and vinegar *(all'agro).*

The Lazio is famous for its Pecorino Romano and Ricotta cheeses. Both have been made here for more than two thousand years. Provatura, Caciocavallo, and Mozzarella cheeses are also produced.

Frascati, one of the wines of the Castelli Romani Hills, is the favorite wine of the Romans. Unfortunately, it does not travel well. Colli Albani is another dry white wine from the same region. Est! Est!! Est!!! di Montefiascone (literally, "big flask," an appropriate name) is probably the most celebrated wine of the Lazio; it is excellent served with pasta.

A Roman meal is not complete without a glass of the famous anisette liqueur, Sambuca. Ask for it *con le mosche* (with flies); these, in fact, are coffee beans, which you crunch while sipping the liqueur.

# LOCAL SPECIALTIES

*CIPOLLINE IN AGRODOLCE:* Onions cooked in sweet-and-sour sauce with tomatoes.

*CARCIOFI ALLA ROMANA:* Artichokes stewed in olive oil, garlic, and mint.

*CARCIOFI ALLA GIUDEA:* Deep-fried artichokes.

*STRACCIATELLA:* Egg drop soup.

*GNOCCHI ALLA ROMANA:* Semolina gnocchi baked with butter and grated cheese.

*FETTUCCINE CON LA RICOTTA:* Egg noodles with ricotta and unsalted butter.

*FETTUCCINE AL BURRO:* Egg noodles with butter and cheese.

*SPAGHETTI ALLA MARINARA:* Spaghetti with a sauce of tomatoes, garlic, olive oil, and hot pepper.

*INSALATA DI MISTICANZA:* A salad of wild greens and herbs, including rocket, sorrel, mint, lamb's lettuce, chicory, and purslane.

*BIETOLE STRASCINATI:* Beet greens or Swiss chard sautéed with garlic and olive oil.

*SPINACI ALLA ROMANA:* Spinach cooked with olive oil, pine nuts, and raisins.

*SUPPLÌ AL TELEFONO:* Rice croquettes stuffed with provatura cheese.

*TORTA DI RICOTTA:* A ricotta cheesecake with lemon rind, vanilla, sugar, and liqueur.

*ZUPPA INGLESE:* Literally, English soup. A rum-soaked cake topped with custard.

## *Abruzzi and Molise*

The Abruzzi and Molise is mountain country, stretching from the Adriatic Sea in the east to some of the highest peaks in the Italian Peninsula. The region is wild and rocky, with some of the most imposing scenery in Italy. Wild bear and wolves still roam in the Abruzzi National Park near Scanno.

Sheep and cattle graze on the high mountain pastures. Scamorza cheese, made from cow's milk, is the most commonly produced cheese but Caciocavallo, Pecorino, Provola, and Ricotta are also made. Cheese is used a great deal in the cooking of the region.

Like the landscape, the cuisine is simple and stark. There is a strong liking for chili peppers, called *diavolillo,* and these flavor many of the local dishes.

The most famous pasta specialty is *maccheroni alla chitarra.* These are homemade egg noodles, cut on a *chitarra,* or wooden frame with steel strings strung across it like a guitar. The noodles are laid over the strings and pressed through so they fall into long thin strands. Most homes in the Abruzzi own a *chitarra.*

The Abruzzi is the only region of Italy where saffron is grown, although it is seldom used in the local cooking; it is exported to Lombardy in the North.

The rocky landscape is not well suited to the cultivation of wine but a few local wines are produced: Cerasuolo d'Abruzzo, a clear red wine that goes well with Scamorza cheese, soups, and vegetables, and Montepulciano d'Abruzzo (red) and Trebbiano d'Abruzzo (white).

## LOCAL SPECIALTIES

*ZUPPA DI CARDI:* Cardoon soup.

*TIMBALLO DI MELANZANE:* A layered pie of fried eggplant, scamorza cheese, and beaten egg.

*CECI DI NAVELLI:* Chick-peas, cooked with onion, olive oil, and rosemary, with cubes of fried bread.

*CARDONI FRITTI ALL'ABRUZZESE:* Cardoon fritters.

*SCRIPPELLE 'MBUSSE:* Pancakes stuffed with peas, pecorino cheese, and a white sauce, topped with tomato and mushroom sauce and baked in the oven.

*FRITTATE CON LE PATATE:* Omelet with potatoes, onions, and hot peppers.

*MACCHERONI CON AGLIO, OLIO E DIAVOLILLIO:* Macaroni with garlic, olive oil, parsley, and hot peppers.

*RAVIOLI ALL'AQUILANA—GRAVIOLI:* Cheese-stuffed ravioli served with sage butter and grated pecorino cheese.

*PAROZZO:* A light cake made with corn flour or potato flour with ground almonds, butter, eggs, and sugar, with a chocolate frosting.

*PEPATELLI:* Cookies made with whole-wheat flour, honey, chopped almonds, grated orange rind, and pepper.

## Campania

Campania is, perhaps, the most beautiful of all the regions of Italy. It is hard to surpass the majesty of the azure Bay of Naples, dominated by Mount Vesuvius, or the magnificent Amalfi Drive with its white Saracen villages set like jewels along its stony cliffs. No wonder that it has been the playground of travelers, artists, poets, and aristocracy for decades.

In contrast, Naples, the second largest port in Italy, is vibrant, noisy, overcrowded, and marked by poverty.

Campania is mainly agricultural. A profusion of fruits and vegetables have grown on the rich volcanic soil since Roman times. The growing season is virtually all year round. Zucchini, eggplant, tomatoes, green beans, cabbage, broccoli, melons, cherries, figs, apples, pears, citrus fruits, grapes, olives, almonds, walnuts, and chestnuts are all cultivated. Some of the most delectable vegetable dishes in Italy are made here.

Naples is most famous for pizza (literally, "pie"). Pizza was made two thousand years ago in Pompeii without tomatoes, of course, which were not introduced to Italy until the sixteenth century.

Naples is also renowned for its macaroni, which it has been manufacturing since the fifteenth century. It is served with colorful and piquant sauces. All over Italy *alla Napoletana* means "with a rich tomato sauce."

Mozzarella cheese is made in the region of Naples. Once it was only made with buffalo's milk, but today a large amount is made with cow's milk, as the buffalo are grazing on more inland pastures. Provola, Provolone, Caciocavallo, and Ricotta are also made here.

Several wines of note are produced in the Naples area. The red Gragnano is the Neapolitans' favorite. Falerno and Lacrima Christi are the most famous wines of the region. Ravello and Capri both produce pleasing dry white wines.


## LOCAL SPECIALTIES

*MINESTRA DI ZUCCHINE:* Zucchini soup.

*INSALATA DI RINFORZO:* Boiled cauliflower with vinaigrette dressing, topped with black olives and capers.

*MELANZANE ALLA PARMIGIANA:* Fried eggplant layered with tomato sauce and mozzarella cheese, baked in the oven; equally good made with zucchini instead of eggplant.

*PATATE ALLA PIZZAIOLA:* Sliced boiled potatoes fried in olive oil with garlic, tomatoes, and herbs.

*PIZZA MARGHERITA:* A classic pizza topped with tomatoes, mozzarella cheese, and herbs.

*CALZONE:* A stuffed pizza in the shape of a "trouser leg."

*MOZZARELLA AI FERRI:* Grilled mozzarella cheese.

*MOZZARELLA IN CARROZZA:* Mozzarella cheese sandwiched between slices of bread and fried in hot oil.

*CRESPOLINI AL FORMAGGIO:* Cheese-filled pancakes.

*LINGUINE ALLA PUTTANESCA:* Linguine with a sauce of tomatoes, black olives, capers, garlic, and hot pepper.

*STRANGULAPRIEVETE:* Literally, "priest strangler." Potato dumplings with tomato sauce.

*PASTIERA:* A rich puff pastry made with grains of wheat boiled in milk, ricotta cheese, and candied fruits.

*ZEPPOLE ALLA NAPOLETANA:* Marsala-flavored fritters.

## Basilicata

Basilicata, or Lucania, as it is sometimes called, is the least visited region in Italy, and the poorest. It has two short coastlines, one to the West, overlooking the Tyrennian Sea tucked between Campania and Calabria, the other on the instep of Italy along the Ionian Sea between Calabria and Apulia.

The terrain is almost totally mountainous. The two main cities are Potenza, which is almost vertical, and the awesome Matera, built between the precipitous slopes of two ravines, with its hodgepodge of houses and ancient cave dwellings hewn out of rock.

Despite the harshness of the land, wheat, vegetables, and fruit, especially citrus fruit, figs, walnuts, chestnuts, olives, and wine grapes are grown wherever possible.

The cooking of Basilicata is simple and austere, based on pasta, vegetables, and legumes, with plenty of garlic, olives, and capers. The people like their food hot. Chili pepper is used in everything from tomato sauce to fried eggs. Several cheeses are produced—a sharp Provolone, Caciocavallo, Scamorza, and Mozzarella, Ricotta and Ricotta Salata, a small, hard goat cheese called Casiddi, and the semi-soft Manteca. The only wine of note is the dry red Aglianico del Vulture, which claims to be the best wine in southern Italy.

## LOCAL SPECIALTIES

*CICORIE E FAVETTE:* Purée of dried beans served with a salad of cooked greens and bread; a specialty of Matera.

*LAÀN:* Tagliatelle with lentils or dried beans.

*MACCHERONI ALLA TRAINIERA:* Macaroni with olive oil, capers, garlic, and hot red pepper.

*LAGANE E CECI:* A kind of tagliatelle, served with chick-peas, olive oil, garlic, and hot red pepper.

*MANDORLATA DI PEPERONI:* Sweet-and-sour peppers with almonds and raisins.

*MOSTACCIOLI:* A primitive cookie made with flour and honey.

*PANZAROTTI:* Deep-fried sweet ravioli stuffed with pureed chickpeas, sugar, chocolate, and cinnamon.

## *Calabria*

Calabria, when it was under Greek rule 2,500 years ago, was the richest region of Italy. The main city was Sybaris on the Ionian coast which later gave its name to the English language, to mean the "epitome of luxury" (and sometimes, degeneracy). Sybaris has disappeared without a trace, but Calabria has more Greek ruins than any other region of Italy, except Sicily.

Today, Calabria is a region plagued by earthquakes and poverty.

The land is harsh and mountainous; the water resources are meager; unemployment is rampant. Many of the young men have been forced to seek employment abroad in order to support their families. Yet, the persevering farmer still grows eggplant, peppers, tomatoes, artichokes, olives, figs, almonds, citrus fruits, and grapes in the more fertile slopes and valleys. Much of the coastline is spectacular. The region is just starting to open up to tourism.

Several cheeses are made: Caciocavallo, Pecorino, Mozzarella, fresh Ricotta, and Ricotta Salata.

Calabrian wines tend to be heavy and strong, and many are used for blending with the subtler wines of northern Italy.

## LOCAL SPECIALTIES

*LICURDIA:* An onion and potato soup flavored with hot pepper and served with croutons.

*MILLECOSEDDE:* A very thick minestrone soup made with a wide variety of dried and fresh vegetables.

*MACCHERONI ALLA PASTORA:* Literally, "shepherd's macaroni"; served with fresh ricotta cheese, butter, and salt.

*MACCHERONI CON CARCIOFI:* Macaroni with artichokes.

*PASTA ASCIUTTA ALLA CALABRESE:* Pasta with tomato sauce and ginger.

*MELANZANE ALL'AGRODOLCE:* Fried eggplant topped with a sweet-and-sour sauce of vinegar, sugar, cinnamon, walnuts, raisins, candied citron, Marsala wine, and chocolate.

*GIANFOTTERE:* A vegetable stew of eggplant, zucchini, tomato, potatoes, onions, herbs, and saffron.

*RIGATONCELLI CON POMODORI:* Tomatoes

stuffed with pasta, flavored with parsley, mint, garlic, and olive oil.

*TURIDDU:* A cookie made of flour, eggs, and almonds.

*CROCETTE:* Figs stuffed with almonds and fennel seeds and lightly roasted in the oven.

## Apulia

Apulia is the spur and heel of the Italian boot, stretching from the Gargano peninsula along the Adriatic Coast to the Ionian Sea. The sun-drenched, whitewashed, cubist towns along the coast are more reminiscent of Greece than Italy.

It is an isolated region, steeped in ancient history, with the remains of a Doric temple at Taranto, the bronze colossus at Barletta, the strange conical roofed *trulli* of Alberobello, and the Norman castle of Castel del Monte, near the town of Andria.

Although Apulia is the richest of the three most southerly regions of Italy, it is still very poor. The northern plains, once providing pasture land for vast herds of sheep, are now mainly used for market gardening. Potatoes, eggplant, artichokes, fennel, fava beans, asparagus, melons, olives, and citrus fruits are all cultivated. The area around Bari produces more wheat and wine than any other region of Italy. However, no great vintages are produced and most of the wine is sent north for blending or for cheap table wine.

The cooking of Apulia is very basic. Bread is the most important staple. Like most of southern Italy, the diet is based on pasta and vegetables. Onions are used more than garlic in cooking. Greens of all kinds are used to stuff pies and *calzoni*, or as an accompaniment to pasta.

A wide selection of local cheeses are made: Cariotta, a whey cheese made in Brindisi, Ricotta, Mozzarella (called Provalina in Bari), Scamorza, and Burrata (which has a butter filling).

Like Calabria, Apulia has wines that are strong, often used for blending with the wines of the North. The best known is probably the white wine of San Severo. Several dessert wines with a high alcoholic content are produced.

# LOCAL SPECIALTIES

**FRISA:** A whole-wheat bun soaked with olive oil and spread with onion and tomato.

**LA CAPRIATA:** A bean purée flavored with olive oil and onions, usually served with a salad of cooked greens.

**MINESTRONE VERDE ALLA BARESE:** A thick green vegetable soup, including turnip tops, Swiss chard, fennel, escarole and, sometimes, cardoons.

**PIZZA RUSTICA ALLA LECCESE:** A two-crust pie made of yeast dough or short-crust pastry. May have a cheese, tomato, or onion filling.

**CALZONE ALLA BARESE:** A stuffed pizza in the shape of a "trouser leg"—filled with sautéed greens, tomatoes, and cheese.

**PANZEROTTI CON RICOTTA ALLA BARESE:** Deep-fried ravioli, stuffed with egg and ricotta cheese.

**RECCHIETELLE ALLA BARESE:** Pasta in the shape of "little ears" served with turnip tops and hot pepper.

**FUSILLI CON LA RUCA:** Fusilli with arugula and tomato sauce.

**TIELLA:** A layered pie of potatoes, onions, vegetables, and herbs, sometimes including rice.

**TARANTO TART:** A flat pie of mashed potatoes, topped with mozzarella cheese and tomatoes and baked in the oven.

*MELANZANE ALLA FOGGIANA:* Stuffed eggplant with olive oil, garlic, tomatoes, bread
crumbs, and herbs.

**FRITTO DI MELANZANE FILANTI:** Fried eggplant and cheese "sandwiches."

**CARTELLATE:** Wine-flavored pastries coated with
honey.

## Sicily

The island of Sicily is Mediterranean in the North and subtropical
in the center and South. The usual Mediterranean vegetables and
fruits are grown: artichokes, eggplant, zucchini, tomatoes, broccoli, sweet peppers, fennel, olives, and capers. The largest amount
of citrus fruits in all Italy is grown in Sicily. There are also grapes,
Smyrna figs, and such exotics as pomegranates, prickly pears,
loquats, and Japanese medlars. Sicily also produces a large amount
of wheat. In fact, it has had a wheat surplus for two thousand years.
No wonder the staples of the poor are bread and macaroni.

The cooking of Sicily is spicy and flavorful or, perhaps I should
say, full of flavors. It is characteristic of Sicilian cooking to have a
multiplicity of tastes in one dish. Sicilian food has some
surprises—a taste of chocolate in a sweet-and-sour eggplant dish,
or a hint of white raisins in a fritter of chopped olives. It is a cuisine
much influenced by the Arabs, especially reflected in the pastries
and sweets, which incorporate honey, sesame seeds, almonds, pistachio nuts, and aniseed.

Sicily produces several cheeses, mainly from ewe's milk. These
include Incanestrato, Caciocavallo (often used for grating when
aged), Pepato, and Ricotta Salata.

Although Sicilian wine is often considered coarser than the
wines of northern Italy, there are some fine wines to be found,
including Corvo (white and red) and Faro (red). The best-known
wine is, of course, Marsala, which may be drunk as an apéritif or
as a dessert wine. Malvasia di Lipari is another noted dessert wine.

# LOCAL SPECIALTIES

*MACCU:* A fava bean purée soup flavored with wild fennel and peperoncini.

*LA CAPONATA:* Fried eggplant and celery in a sweet-and-sour sauce with olives and capers.

*FRITEDDA:* Artichokes, peas, and fava beans cooked in a sweet-and-sour sauce.

*BROCCOLI ALLA SICILIANA:* Broccoli cooked with cheese, black olives, and wine.

*PANELLE:* Chick-pea fritters.

*MACCHERONI ALLA PAOLINA:* Macaroni with cabbage, pine nuts, and raisins.

*SPAGHETTI ALLA SIRACUSANA:* Spaghetti with a sauce of tomato, garlic, eggplant, sweet pepper, olives, and capers.

*LA SCACCIA:* Pasta baked in a pie shell with broccoli, tomato, and cheese.

*MILLASSATA:* A *frittata* (omelet), with artichoke hearts, asparagus tips, parsley, and grated cheese.

*CRISPEDDE:* Ricotta fritters; a specialty of Catania.

*CANNOLI:* Cylinders of pastry, usually filled with ricotta cheese, candied fruits, chopped nuts, and liqueur.

*CASSATA (cake):* A spongecake filled with ricotta cheese, flavored with Maraschino, candied fruit, chocolate, and whipped cream.

*CASSATA (ice cream):* A multicolored ice cream flavored with liqueurs, candied fruits, and grated chocolate.

# Sardinia

D. H. Lawrence wrote of Sardinia: "So different from Sicily; none of the suave Greek Italian charms, none of the airs and graces, none of the glamour. Rather bare, rather stark, sometimes like Malta but without Malta's liveliness . . . lost between Europe and Africa."

Sardinia is the second largest island in the Mediterranean (Sicily is the largest). The landscape is mainly mountainous, barren, treeless, and windswept. Sheep graze on the hills and plains. The population is sparse. The winters are mild and the summers are hot and parched.

Vegetables generally do not grow well, but eggplant, zucchini, white and purple cauliflower, peas, fennel (often wild), fava and string beans are cultivated, and artichokes thrive. Fruits, including pomegranates, prickly pears, cherries, figs, melons, and citrus fruits are plentiful, as are walnuts, almonds, hazelnuts, and chestnuts.

Bread is the staple food, especially *carasau* or *carta di musica* (music paper bread)—crisp, thin, round sheets resembling tortillas. The Sardinians prefer bread to pasta, although they do make their own pasta, gnocchi, and polenta.

Sardinians are fond of cakes and pastries, especially when made with almonds, honey, and dried fruits.

Several cheeses are produced; the famous Pecorino Sardo (so beloved by the Ligurians), Fiore Sardo, Caciocavallo, and Fetta, which is similar to the Greek feta cheese.

The wines of Sardinia are inclined to be sweet and heavy. Vernaccia is the best-known wine, and often drunk as an apéritif. Vermentino di Gallura and Nasco are fine white dessert wines.

## LOCAL SPECIALTIES

***ZUPPA DI FINOCHIETTI SELVATICI:*** A cross between a soup and a casserole; layers of boiled fennel, toasts, and fresh pecorino cheese in broth, all baked in the oven.

***ZUPPA SARDA:*** A broth, thickened with eggs,

mozzarella cheese, parsley, and grated cheese, poured over toasts.

*LA CAULEDDA:* Cauliflower soup.

*LA FAVATA:* Fava bean soup.

*CULINGIONES:* Ravioli stuffed with spinach, fresh cheese, eggs, and saffron, usually served with tomato sauce.

*MACCARONES A FERRITUS CON AGLIO E OLIO:* Homemade noodles with tomato sauce, flavored with garlic, olive oil, and hot pepper (*peperoncini*).

*CULURIONES:* Potato ravioli, stuffed with onion, mint, egg, and grated pecorino cheese, served with tomato sauce.

*FAGIOLI ALLA GALLURESE:* Dried white beans cooked with olive oil, garlic, tomato, fennel, onion, and cabbage.

*CARDI ALLA SARDA:* Boiled cardoons dressed with boiled egg, parsley, olive oil, melted butter, and bread crumbs.

*TORTA DI PISELLI:* A baked pea omelet.

*TURTA DI FAISCEDDA:* A sweet fava bean omelet.

*SOSPIRI:* Almond meringues.

*ARANZATA DI NUORO:* Orange peel, candied in honey and mixed with toasted almonds.

*PABASSINOS:* A diamond-shaped cookie studded with raisins, almonds, and walnuts.

*ABUFAUS:* A kind of gingerbread made with honey, pine nuts, walnuts, currants, and spices.

# ANTIPASTI AND SALADS

֍֍֍

## ANTIPASTI E INSALATE

"Salad refreshes without fatiguing and strengthens without irritating. I usually say it renews one's youth."—Brillat-Savarin, *The Physiology of Taste*

The Italians have created some of the most varied and imaginative antipasti or hors-d'oeuvre in Europe. Fortunately, most of the dishes are easy to prepare. Antipasti made in the home are generally very simple. A typical antipasto might consist of one or two marinated vegetables, some olives, a small plate of tomato salad with a few slices of cheese or a stuffed egg on the side. Antipasto literally means "before the meal" so always keep the quantities small. The purpose is to whet the appetite, not to satisfy it.

Most regions of Italy serve some form of pickled or marinated vegetables as an antipasto. Some are simply boiled in vinegar and spices and dressed with olive oil, some are marinated in wine and herbs, others are cooked in a sweet-and-sour sauce.

In northern Italy, especially in the Alpine regions, there are various forms of cheese dips and spreads that are served with toasts or vegetables. In the South, where fewer dairy products are available, these cheese dishes are replaced by bean dips and spreads.

Crisp, raw salads or salads of cooked vegetables are often eaten before the meal. Most restaurants and trattorie in Rome serve cooked salads of dark green leafy vegetables dressed with olive oil, lemon juice, and garlic. Farther south these cooked salads are often spiced with hot red pepper *(peperoncini)*.

Rice salads are often served at the beginning of the meal in northern Italy. There are many variations. Artichoke hearts, asparagus, mushrooms, truffles, fennel, celery, sweet peppers, olives, capers, raisins, and pine nuts all make excellent additions.

Virgin olive oil and a good quality wine vinegar (or lemon juice) are essential to making good antipasti and salads. Mustard or cream is rarely used in Italian dressings except in Piedmont and Lombardy, where the French culinary influence is still strong. Mayonnaise and flavored mayonnaise are used throughout Italy.

Many dishes found elsewhere in this book, especially some of the stuffed vegetables and fritters, cheese *crostini,* and some vegetable dishes, make excellent antipasti. The Italians make no distinction between a vegetable entrée or an antipasto. It is just the size of the dish that determines whether it is an antipasto, a main course, or a vegetable accompaniment.

*L o m b a r d y*

## MIXED VEGETABLES IN VINEGAR
### (Giardinetto di sott'aceto)

Pickled vegetables or *sott'aceti* are made all over Italy. Onions, carrots, and green beans make a colorful combination. Other vegetables suitable for pickling are mushrooms, cauliflower, artichoke hearts, young cucumbers, fennel, and beets. Try to use an imported wine vinegar as it is much milder than domestic wine vinegar.

½ pound small white onions
½ pound young tender carrots, diced
½ pound green beans, cut into 1-inch lengths
1½ cups wine vinegar
1½ cups water
3 tablespoons olive oil
2 bay leaves
6 whole cloves
1 tablespoon fresh basil leaves, or ½ teaspoon dried
6 black peppercorns

Combine all the ingredients in a saucepan. Bring to a boil, cover, and simmer for 10 minutes, or until the vegetables are just tender. Do not overcook. The vegetables should still be crisp. Remove the vegetables with a slotted spoon and set aside. Raise the heat and reduce the liquid to about 2 cups. Place the vegetables in a bowl and pour the reduced liquid over them. Make sure the liquid covers the vegetables. Refrigerate for at least 12 hours before serving. *Serves 6.*

*Liguria*

## MARINATED MUSHROOMS
### *(Funghi marinati)*

1 pound mushrooms, sliced
1 cup dry white wine
1 bay leaf
1 garlic clove, crushed
3 peppercorns
1 -inch cinnamon stick

¹/₈  teaspoon freshly grated nutmeg
     Pinch of rosemary
¹/₄  cup olive oil

Combine the mushrooms, wine, bay leaf, garlic, and peppercorns in a saucepan. Bring to a boil and simmer for 5 minutes. Add the cinnamon stick, nutmeg, and rosemary and simmer for 5 minutes more. Place in a serving bowl, cover with olive oil, and chill for at least 12 hours before serving. *Serves 6.*

*Piedmont*

## ARTICHOKES WITH EGG AND WINE SAUCE
*(Carciofi allo zabaglione)*

———— 🌿🌿🌿 ————

4    globe artichokes
4    egg yolks
1    teaspoon warm water
¹/₂  cup dry white wine
2    tablespoons butter, softened

Trim the stems of the artichokes. Steam the vegetables for 45 minutes to 1 hour, or until the bottoms are tender when pierced with a sharp knife and the outer leaves pull away easily. Set aside to cool.

Place the egg yolks and warm water in the top pan of a double boiler over hot, not boiling, water. Beat with a wire whisk until the mixture becomes foamy. Slowly pour in the white wine in a thin trickle, whisking constantly until the mixture forms soft mounds. Beat in the softened butter. Pour this sauce into 4 individual pots. Arrange the artichokes on individual platters and serve at once with a pot of sauce on the side. *Serves 4.*

*Alto Adige*

## ASPARAGUS WITH HARD-BOILED EGG SAUCE
### *(Asparagi alla salsa Bolzanina)*

This recipe is from Bolzano in the Alto Adige. Sometimes capers are added to give a more piquant sauce.

2   pounds asparagus
2   hard-boiled eggs
2   egg yolks
1   teaspoon Dijon mustard
2   tablespoons lemon juice
1   cup sunflowerseed oil
1   tablespoon fresh chives, chopped
1   teaspoon fresh tarragon, chopped
    Salt
    Freshly ground black pepper

Trim the ends of the asparagus and with a sharp knife remove any fibrous inedible parts from the lower stalks. Steam for 15 to 20 minutes or until tender.

Meanwhile separate the yolks from the whites of the hard-boiled eggs, and place them in a mixing bowl with the raw egg yolks, the mustard, and a few drops of lemon juice. Mix well together. Very slowly beat in the oil, drop by drop, with a wire whisk. When the mixture becomes very thick, thin it with a few drops of lemon juice. When the oil is used up, stir in the finely chopped hard-boiled egg whites and the herbs. Season to taste with salt and black pepper. Arrange the asparagus on individual plates and serve with the sauce on the side. *Serves 4.*

*Veneto*

## VENETIAN PEPERONATA
### *(Peperonata alla veneta)*

The Venetian version of this famous Florentine dish includes eggplant, and uses dry white
wine instead of wine vinegar. Sometimes
olives and capers are included.

6   green or yellow sweet peppers
1   small eggplant, about ¼ pound
⅓  cup olive oil
1   garlic clove, crushed
1   large onion, thinly sliced
1   cup canned plum tomatoes, seeded and
    chopped
3   tablespoons dry white wine
    Salt
    Freshly ground black pepper

Remove ribs and seeds from the sweet peppers and cut peppers
into strips. Cut the unpeeled eggplant into ½-inch cubes.

Heat the olive oil in a large frying pan and cook the garlic and onion
over moderate heat for 3 minutes. Add the eggplant and peppers
and continue to cook, covered, for 15 minutes, or until eggplant
and peppers are just tender, stirring occasionally so the vegetables
cook evenly. Add the tomatoes, cover, and simmer for 20 minutes,
or until the sauce is thickened. Add the wine, raise the heat
slightly, and cook for 5 minutes longer. The *peperonata* should be
fairly dry at the end of cooking. Season with salt and pepper to
taste. May be served hot or cold. *Serves 6.*

*Sicily*

# LA CAPONATA, CATANIA STYLE
### *(La caponata catanese)*

*La caponata,* or *caponatina,* is Sicily's most famous antipasto. Its ingredients vary around the island. Artichoke hearts, potatoes, and hard-cooked eggs are all possible additions. In Syracuse it is made with grated chocolate instead of tomato sauce.

| | |
|---|---|
| 1 | large eggplant |
| ⅔ | cup olive oil |
| 1 | medium-size onion, chopped |
| 1 | celery rib, chopped |
| 1 | sweet red pepper, cut into small dice |
| ¾ | cup canned tomatoes, forced through a sieve or puréed in the blender |
| 2 | tablespoons white raisins |
| 2 | tablespoons pine nuts |
| ¼ | cup green olives, pitted and sliced |
| 2 | tablespoons capers |
| 3 | tablespoons wine vinegar |
| 1 | tablespoon sugar or honey |
| | Salt |
| | Freshly ground black pepper |

Wash the eggplant but do not peel it. Cut into ½-inch cubes. Heat the olive oil in a large frying pan and cook the eggplant over moderate heat until it is soft and starting to turn golden. Remove from the pan. Add remaining olive oil and cook the onion for 5 minutes, or until they are soft. Add the celery and sweet pepper and continue to cook until they are soft. Add the tomato purée and cook over moderate heat for 8 to 10 minutes, until the sauce starts to thicken. Stir in the raisins, pine nuts, olives, capers, vinegar, and sugar. Simmer for 5 minutes to blend the flavors. Add the cooked eggplant, stir well, and season with salt and black pepper. Cover and simmer for 10 minutes, stirring often to prevent scorching. Transfer to a serving dish and serve at room temperature. *Serves 4 to 6.*

*Liguria*

## Eggs Stuffed with Pesto
*(Uova ripiene col pesto)*

6 hard-cooked eggs
¹/₄ cup Pesto Sauce (page 62)
¹/₄ cup mayonnaise
Salt
Freshly ground black pepper
1 tablespoon capers

Cut eggs lengthwise into halves. Remove yolks and mash in a bowl. Blend in the pesto sauce, mayonnaise, and salt and black pepper to taste. Spoon the mixture into the egg halves and garnish with capers. *Serves 6.*

*Friuli and Venezia Giulia*

## Liptauer Cheese, Friuli Style
*(Liptauer friulana)*

This recipe dates back to the turn of the century when Friuli was part of the Austro-Hungarian Empire. If you prefer, the kümmel can be replaced by single cream.

3 tablespoons butter, softened
1 cup Ricotta cheese
1 or 2 tablespoons kümmel or brandy
2 tablespoons minced onion
1 teaspoon capers, chopped
1 teaspoon Dijon mustard
1 teaspoon paprika
  Pinch of ground cumin
  Salt
4 to 6 slices of rye bread, toasted

Beat the butter in a mixing bowl until it is soft and light. Gradually add the Ricotta cheese and blend well until very smooth. Thin with enough kümmel to give a spreading consistency—the mixture should not be too soft or soupy. Add the next 5 ingredients and blend well. Form into a mound on a serving platter. Sprinkle with a little additional paprika and serve with slices of rye toast. *Serves 4 to 6.*

*L o m b a r d y*

## GORGONZOLA TOASTS
### (Crostini di gorgonzola)

Perfect with a bottle of dry red wine.

¼ pound Gorgonzola cheese
¼ pound butter, softened
2 tablespoons brandy
6 slices of whole-wheat bread, toasted

Crumble the Gorgonzola cheese into a mixing bowl. Add the softened butter and mix well. Blend in the brandy. Cut the toasts diagonally into quarters, and spread with the cheese mixture. *Serves 6.*

*A p u l i a*

## LA CAPRIATA
### (La capriata)

————— ❦❦❦ —————

*La capriata* is a simple fava bean purée. It is usually served with a salad of cooked turnip tops dressed with plenty of garlic and virgin olive oil. It is also found in Basilicata and parts of Calabria. The dish dates back to the days when most of southern Italy was under Greek rule. Use shelled fava beans, which are available in Italian groceries and gourmet shops.

1   cup dried fava beans
3   cups water
1   small onion, coarsely chopped
4   tablespoons virgin olive oil
    Salt
    Cayenne pepper
4   slices of whole wheat bread, toasted

Soak the beans in water overnight and drain.

Bring beans to a boil in 3 cups of water and add the onion. Cover and simmer for 1½ to 2 hours, or until the beans are very tender and most of the liquid is evaporated.

Force the beans and onion through a sieve or purée in a blender. Add half the olive oil and season with salt to taste. The consistency should be very creamy.

Transfer to a serving bowl. Pour over the remaining olive oil and sprinkle lightly with cayenne pepper. Serve at room temperature with slices of toast on the side. *Serves 4.*

## Olives and Olive Oil
### *(Olive e olio d'oliva)*

Olive trees have long been a symbol of wealth in the Mediterranean. They have been cultivated in Italy since Roman times, when bread and olives were a staple food of the peasants.

An olive tree has a life span of 300 to 700 years, though some olive trees have been said to live a thousand years. They thrive on well-drained soil in full sun and can survive for more than six months without water.

The unripe green olives are picked in the autumn, soaked in a lye solution to remove their bitterness, and then pickled in brine. If left on the tree, they ripen and turn jet black by December and are then picked for marinating or crushing into oil.

The best quality olive oil is virgin olive oil, cold-pressed from the first pressing. It has a rich green color and a strong fruity flavor. It is probably the most healthy of all fruit oils as olives can be pressed easily without using heat or chemicals. *It has the additional benefit of having no cholesterol.* Peasants in southern Italy who consume vast quantities of olive oil (up to one fifth of their daily diet) have been found to have very low levels of blood cholesterol.

Olive oil keeps best in a cool dry place. It should not be kept in the refrigerator as it will coagulate.

*L a z i o*

## CELERY IN PINZIMONIO
*(Sedani in Pinzimonio)*

Romans love to eat raw vegetables dipped into virgin olive oil. It is the perfect start to a meal. Nothing could be better for health or digestion. Try it with radishes, fennel, sweet pepper, cucumber, or carrot sticks.

1   bunch of celery
1   cup virgin olive oil
1   garlic clove, crushed
    Salt
    Pinch of hot red pepper flakes

Trim the celery, cut into 4-inch lengths, and arrange in a serving dish. Pour the olive oil into a small serving bowl and mix with the garlic and salt and hot red pepper to taste. *Serves 4 to 6.*

*Valle d'Aosta*

# RADISH AND GRUYÈRE SALAD
*(Insalata di ravanelli e groviera)*

    2  cups sliced radishes
    2  ounces Gruyère cheese, cut into small dice
   ¼  cup Italian or Greek black olives, pitted
       and sliced
   ½  cup Vinaigrette Sauce (page 65)

Combine the radish slices, Gruyère cheese, and black olives in a
salad bowl. Pour the vinaigrette sauce over them and toss well.
*Serves 3 to 4.*

*Lazio*

# ROMAN MIXED SALAD
*(Insalata di misticanza)*

In Rome, *insalata di misticanza* consists of at least
15 different salad greens and herbs, usually including rocket, sorrel, lamb's lettuce, puslane, curly
endive, chicory, dandelion, mint, basil, and val-
erian. *Misticanza* is the Roman name for rocket.

   ½  bunch of arugula
   ¼  pound lamb's lettuce
   ¼  pound red chicory
   ¼  pound spinach
   ½  bunch watercress
   ¼  curly endive
    1  small fennel bulb, diced

2  green onions, thinly sliced
1  handful of fresh parsley, chopped
1  handful of fresh mint, chopped
2  tablespoons fresh chives, chopped
⅓  cup Vinaigrette Sauce (page 65)

Break the arugula, lamb's lettuce, red chicory, spinach, watercress, and endive into bite-size pieces. Place in a salad bowl with the fennel, green onions, parsley, mint, basil, and chives. Pour over the vinaigrette sauce, toss lightly, and serve at once. *Serves 4 to 6.*

*Veneto*

## RED CHICORY SALAD
### (Insalata di radicchio rosso)

Red chicory or *radicchio rosso* is the most highly prized salad "green" in Italy. It is grown in the region around Treviso and is only available in the winter months. It has beautiful reddish-purple leaves, marbled with white, and a unique, slightly bitter taste. It is well worth searching out in Italian groceries. If unavailable, curly endive may be used instead.

1  head red chicory or curly endive
1  Bermuda onion, thinly sliced
2  large tomatoes, peeled and sliced
½  leek, thinly sliced
1  handful of parsley, finely chopped
⅓  cup Vinaigrette Sauce (page 65)

Break the red chicory into bite-size pieces. Place in a salad bowl with the onion, tomatoes, leek, and parsley. Pour the vinaigrette sauce over the salad, toss lightly, and serve at once. *Serves 4.*

*Lazio*

## SWISS CHARD SALAD
### (Insalata di bietole)

The Romans love salads of cooked green vegetables dressed with olive oil, lemon juice, and
garlic. Green beans, broccoli, beet greens, and
spinach are all served the same way. Always
dress the vegetables while they are still warm.

    2   large bunches of Swiss chard
    3   tablespoons olive oil
    1   tablespoon lemon juice
    2   garlic cloves, crushed
        Salt
        Freshly ground black pepper

Wash the Swiss chard and remove the thick ribs. Steam in a covered saucepan for 6 to 8 minutes, or until tender. Drain well and
let cool slightly. Place in a salad bowl and dress with olive oil,
lemon juice, garlic, and salt and black pepper to taste. Toss lightly
and serve. *Serves 4 to 6.*

*Liguria*

## MIXED SALAD LIGURIAN STYLE
### (Condijon)

    6   large tomatoes, peeled and sliced
    6   green onions, thinly sliced

1   yellow or green sweet pepper, cut into
thin strips
½   cucumber, peeled and thinly sliced
8   radishes, sliced
12  black olives
1   teaspoon capers
2   hard-cooked eggs, quartered
⅓   cup Vinaigrette Sauce (page 65)

Combine all the vegetables in a salad bowl. Add the olives, capers, quartered eggs, and vinaigrette sauce. Toss well and serve at once. *Serves 6.*

*Lombardy*

## LETTUCE AND GORGONZOLA SALAD
### *(Insalata di lattuga e gorgonzola)*

This simple salad of lettuce and chopped walnuts is tossed with a delicious dressing of Gorgonzola cheese, vinaigrette sauce, cream, and tarragon.

1   head of lettuce
¼   cup shelled walnuts, coarsely chopped
¼   cup Gorgonzola cheese
⅓   cup Vinaigrette Sauce (page 65)
3   tablespoons light cream
1   teaspoon fresh tarragon leaves, or ½
teaspoon dried

Break the lettuce into bite-size pieces and place in a salad bowl with the chopped walnuts. Mash the Gorgonzola cheese with a fork in a bowl. Gradually blend in the vinaigrette sauce, cream, and tarragon until the sauce is smooth and creamy. Pour over the lettuce and walnuts, toss lightly, and serve at once. *Serves 4 to 6.*

*Piedmont*

## MUSHROOM, CELERY, AND PARMESAN CHEESE SALAD WITH BRANDY CREAM DRESSING
### (Insalata di funghi alla torinese)

※ ※ ※

A specialty of Torino.

 2 tablespoons olive oil
 1 pound button mushrooms, sliced
 1 tablespoon water
 2 cups thinly sliced celery
 1/2 cup slivers of Parmesan cheese
 2 tablespoons sliced, pitted green olives
 1/2 cup Vinaigrette Sauce (page 65), made with lemon juice
 2 tablespoons light cream
 1 teaspoon brandy
   Salt
   Freshly ground black pepper
 1 truffle, sliced paper-thin

Heat the olive oil in a large frying pan. Add the mushrooms and 1 tablespoon water and cook over moderate heat for 5 minutes. Drain away any excess liquid and let the mushrooms cool.

Combine the celery, mushrooms, Parmesan cheese, and olives in a salad bowl. Combine the vinaigrette sauce with the cream, brandy, and salt and black pepper to taste. Pour over the salad and toss lightly. Garnish with the truffle. Serve at once. *Serves 4.*

*Piedmont*

## SWEET PEPPER AND FONTINA CHEESE SALAD
### *(Insalata di fontina)*

This traditional Piedmontese salad is served in the late summer and autumn when sweet peppers are ripe and plentiful. The sweet peppers are combined with fontina cheese and green olives and mixed with a deliciously light mustard and cream dressing.

 6   yellow or red sweet peppers
 6   ounces fontina cheese, cut into small dice
10   green olives, pitted and sliced
 1   teaspoon Dijon-style mustard
 2   tablespoons light cream
1/3  cup olive oil
 1   teaspoon lemon juice
 1   teaspoon fresh tarragon leaves, or 1/2
     teaspoon dried
     Salt
     Freshly ground black pepper

Roast the sweet peppers under the broiler until the skins are blackened all over. Wash off the skins under cold water. Pat dry and cut into thin strips. Place in a salad bowl with the fontina cheese and green olives. Mix the mustard and cream together in a bowl. Blend in the olive oil, lemon juice, and tarragon. Pour over the pepper mixture, and season with salt and pepper to taste. Toss well and serve. *Serves 6.*

*L a z i o*

# MOZZARELLA WITH TOMATOES AND BLACK OLIVES
### (Mozzarella con pomodori e olive neri)

Fresh mozzarella should be used for this recipe.

| | |
|---|---|
| 12 | ounces fresh mozzarella cheese |
| 4 | large tomatoes |
| 1/4 | cup olive oil |
| 1 | tablespoon fresh basil, or 1/2 teaspoon dried |
| 20 | black olives |
| | Salt |
| | Freshly ground black pepper |

Cut the mozzarella and tomatoes into slices 1/4 inch thick. Arrange the mozzarella on individual plates and top with slices of tomato. Pour a little olive oil over the top and sprinkle with fresh basil. Garnish with black olives and season with salt and black pepper to taste. *Serves 4.*

*Sicily*

## STUFFED TOMATOES WITH VEGETABLES AND MAYONNAISE
### (Insalata Siciliana)

6  large ripe tomatoes
1  cup Marinated Mushrooms (page 35)
1  cucumber, cut into small dice
3  celery ribs, thinly sliced
1  cup cooked green beans, cut into ½-inch
   lengths
1  tablespoon capers
½  cup mayonnaise
18  black olives

Slice the top quarter off the tomatoes. Reserve the tops for lids. Combine the mushrooms, cucumber, celery, green beans, and capers in a bowl. Spoon the mayonnaise over the mixed vegetables and toss lightly. Spoon some of the mixture into each tomato and replace the reserved lids. Arrange on a serving platter and surround with remaining mixed vegetables. Garnish with black olives and serve. *Serves 6.*

*Campania*

## FAVA BEAN SALAD
### (Insalata di fave)

This is a specialty of Naples.

> 2 cups shelled fava beans
> 1 teaspoon fresh mint leaves, chopped, or ¼
> teaspoon dried mint
> ½ cup Vinaigrette Sauce (page 65)

Bring the fava beans to a boil in lightly salted water and cook, covered, for 45 to 50 minutes, or until they are tender. Drain and place in a serving bowl. Mix the fresh mint with the vinaigrette sauce and pour over the beans while they are still hot. Toss lightly. Serve warm or at room temperature. *Serves 3 or 4.*

*Sicily*

## COUNTRY BEAN AND POTATO SALAD
### (Insalata alla contadina)

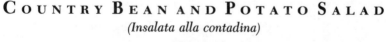

This hearty salad is perfect for a buffet.

> 1 pound new potatoes, boiled and diced
> 1 pound green beans, steamed and cut into
> 1-inch lengths
> 1½ cups cooked dried white beans
> 1 small onion, finely chopped

> ¹⁄₄ cup Italian or Greek black olives, pitted and sliced
> 1 tablespoon capers
> 1 cup Vinaigrette Sauce (page 65)
> 2 tablespoons finely chopped fresh parsley

Combine the potatoes, green beans, cooked white beans, onion, black olives, and capers in a salad bowl. Pour the vinaigrette sauce over the salad and toss well. Sprinkle with parsley. Serve at room temperature. *Serves 6.*

*Sicily*

## POTATO SALAD WITH MARSALA
### (Insalata di patate)

> 2 pounds waxy potatoes, boiled and sliced
> 2 tablespoons dry Marsala wine
> 1 onion, chopped
> 2 celery ribs, thinly sliced
> 2 teaspoons chopped fresh basil
> 2 tablespoons finely chopped fresh parsley
> ²⁄₃ cup Vinaigrette Sauce (page 65)

Place the potatoes in a salad bowl and sprinkle with the wine while they are still warm. Add the onion, celery, basil, parsley, and vinaigrette sauce. Toss lightly and serve. *Serves 6.*

*Piedmont*

## PIEDMONTESE RICE SALAD
*(Insalata di riso alla piemontese)*

There are many versions of rice salad in northern Italy. Raisins, capers, sliced gherkins, artichoke hearts, marinated mushrooms, radishes, fennel, and tomatoes all make excellent additions.

4   cups cooked rice
¼   pound asparagus tips, cooked
1   cup thinly sliced celery
1   sweet red pepper, diced
2   green onions, thinly sliced
⅓   cup homemade Mayonnaise (page 66)
1   teaspoon Dijon-style mustard
1   teaspoon fresh marjoram, or ¼ teaspoon
     dried
1   teaspoon dry Marsala wine
2   tablespoons pitted and sliced green olives
1   truffle, sliced paper-thin (optional)

Combine the rice, asparagus, celery, sweet pepper, and green onions in a salad bowl. Mix the mayonnaise with the mustard, marjoram, and Marsala and pour over the salad. Toss lightly. Garnish with the green olives and truffle. Chill for 1 to 2 hours before serving. *Serves 6.*

# SAUCES

🙰🙰🙰

## SALSE

Italian food is not served in sauces like French food. A few simple sauces are used to enhance the natural flavor of the food.

Tomato sauce has become synonymous with Italian cooking, especially in the United States, but tomato sauce is rarely used in northern Italian cooking. While tomato sauce predominates in the cooking of the South, the flavoring varies from region to region. In Basilicata, the sauce is highly spiced with ginger. Many areas of the South, especially in Apulia, add *peperoncini,* hot pungent chili peppers. In Sicily, olives, capers, raisins, and pine nuts may be added, producing a strong sweet-and-sour flavor. In Liguria, fresh or dried mushrooms are often added to tomato sauce to make the local sauce called *tocco di funghi.*

Liguria is more famous for its green sauces, the basil sauce, *pesto,* and *salsa di noci,* a parsley and walnut sauce.

Emilia-Romagna claims to have invented the classic white béchamel or *balsamella* sauce as far back as the fourteenth century. (This is still disputed by the French, who claim it was invented by Louis XIV's chef.) Béchamel sauce is a basic ingredient of many dishes all over Italy, especially lasagne, *timballi, sformati,* and many gratins.

Fundamental to Italian cooking, but not strictly a sauce, is the *soffritto* or *battuto.* This is a finely chopped combination of garlic, onion, celery, carrot, and herbs that is quickly sautéed in olive oil, or olive oil and butter. The *soffritto* is the foundation of many Italian soups and stews.

*Campania*

## TOMATO SAUCE
### *(La Pommarola)*

※ ※ ※

This is my favorite tomato sauce. It is very light, still tastes of tomatoes, and takes less than 15 minutes to prepare.

2 tablespoons olive oil
1 garlic clove, crushed
1 tablespoon fresh basil, or ½ teaspoon dried
2 tablespoons finely chopped fresh parsley
3 cups canned plum tomatoes, seeded and chopped
   Salt
   Freshly ground black pepper

Heat the olive oil in a large frying pan and cook the garlic, basil, and parsley for 1 minute. Add the chopped tomatoes and salt and black pepper to taste. Cook, uncovered, over high heat for 8 to 10 minutes, or until the sauce starts to thicken, mashing the tomatoes gently with a fork as they cook. *Enough sauce for 1 pound of pasta.*

*Campania and the South*

# TOMATO SAUCE WITH OLIVES AND CAPERS
*(La pizzaiola)*

Hot and piquant

3  tablespoons olive oil
2  garlic cloves, crushed
1/8  teaspoon hot red pepper flakes
1  teaspoon fresh oregano, or 1/4 teaspoon dried
3  cups canned plum tomatoes, seeded and chopped
1/4  cup Italian or Greek black olives, pitted and roughly chopped
2  tablespoons capers
   Salt

Heat the olive oil in a large frying pan and cook the garlic, hot pepper, and oregano for 1 minute. Add the chopped tomatoes, olives, capers, and salt to taste. Cook, uncovered, over high heat for 8 to 10 minutes, or until the sauce starts to thicken, mashing the tomatoes gently with a fork as they cook. *Enough sauce for 1 pound of pasta.*

*L a z i o*

# TOMATO SAUCE WITH WINE
### *(Sugo finto)*

This tomato sauce is cooked more slowly and is richly flavored with vegetables and wine.

¼  cup olive oil
1  garlic clove, crushed
1  tablespoon finely chopped fresh parsley
1  teaspoon fresh marjoram, or ¼ teaspoon dried
1  medium-size onion, finely chopped
1  celery rib, finely sliced
1  small carrot, finely chopped
1  whole clove
⅓  cup dry white wine
3  cups canned plum tomatoes, seeded and chopped
   Salt
   Freshly ground black pepper

Heat the olive oil in a large frying pan and cook the garlic, parsley, and marjoram for 1 minute. Add the onion, celery, carrot, and clove and cook gently for 8 to 10 minutes, or until the vegetables start to soften. Add the wine and cook over high heat until it has almost evaporated. Add the tomatoes and salt and black pepper to taste, and continue cooking over moderate heat for 20 to 30 minutes, or until the sauce has thickened. Pass through a food mill. Return to the pan and heat through. *Enough sauce for 1 pound of pasta.*

*Liguria*

## MUSHROOM AND TOMATO SAUCE
### *(Tocco di funghi)*

1/4  cup olive oil
4    garlic cloves, crushed
1    handful of fresh parsley, finely chopped
1    teaspoon fresh marjoram, or 1/4 teaspoon
     dried
1    pound fresh mushrooms, thinly sliced
2    cups canned plum tomatoes, seeded and
     chopped
     Salt
     Freshly ground black pepper

Heat the olive oil in a large frying pan and cook the garlic, parsley, and marjoram for 1 minute. Add the sliced mushrooms and cook over moderate heat for 5 minutes or until they are tender. Add the tomatoes and salt and black pepper to taste and cook over high heat for 8 to 10 minutes, or until the sauce starts to thicken, mashing the tomatoes gently with a fork as they cook. *Enough sauce for 1 pound of pasta.*

*Emilia-Romagna*

## BÉCHAMEL SAUCE
### (La balsamella)

This recipe makes a medium-thick béchamel sauce that is especially good for lasagne. For a thinner sauce simply add more milk until you have the desired consistency.

    4   tablespoons butter
    3   tablespoons flour
    2   cups hot milk
    ½   teaspoon salt
        Pinch of white pepper
    ¼   teaspoon freshly grated nutmeg

Melt the butter in a heavy-bottomed pan. Stir in the flour and cook for 1 minute without browning. Pour in a little hot milk and stir vigorously with a wooden spoon until the mixture is thick and free of lumps. Gradually add more milk until all the milk is incorporated and the sauce is very smooth and creamy. Season with salt, pepper, and nutmeg and simmer for 1 or 2 more minutes. *Makes about 1 pint.*

## PINE NUTS
### (Pignoli)

Pine nuts or *pignoli* come from the stone pine *(Pinus pinea)*, a native Italian tree. They are soft cream-colored nuts, not unlike almonds in flavor. They are frequently used in Italian stuffings, rice dishes, sauces, and confectionery, and are also one of the basic ingredients of the famous Ligurian sauce, *pesto alla genovese*. They are a very good additional source of protein for vegetarians.

*Liguria*

# PESTO SAUCE
### (Pesto alla genovese)

—————— ❧❧❧ ——————

This famous Ligurian sauce is traditionally made with a mortar and pestle, but a blender makes a perfect sauce in a fraction of the time. *Pesto* is used as a sauce for pasta and gnocchi, to enrich vegetable soups, and with stuffed eggs.

- 2 cups fresh basil leaves
- 1 handful of fresh parsley
- 1 teaspoon fresh marjoram, or 1/4 teaspoon dried
- 2 garlic cloves, crushed
- 1/3 cup olive oil
- 3 tablespoons pine nuts
- 1/3 cup freshly grated pecorino sardo or Parmesan cheese

Place the basil, parsley, marjoram, garlic, olive oil, and pine nuts in a blender and mix slowly until the ingredients are chopped. Add 2 or 3 tablespoons of hot water and the grated cheese. Blend at high speed until the mixture is smooth. *Enough for 1 1/2 to 2 pounds of pasta.*

*L i g u r i a*

### SPINACH PESTO
*(Pesto con spinaci)*

Spinach makes a delicious *pesto* when fresh
basil is unavailable.

2 cups fresh spinach leaves
1/2 cup fresh parsley
2 tablespoons pine nuts
10 shelled walnut halves
2 garlic cloves, crushed
1/3 cup olive oil
1/2 cup freshly grated pecorino sardo or
Parmesan cheese

Place the spinach, parsley, pine nuts, walnuts, garlic, and olive oil
in a blender and mix slowly until the ingredients are chopped. Add
2 or 3 tablespoons of hot water and the grated cheese. Blend at
high speed until the mixture is smooth. *Enough for 1 1/2 to 2 pounds
of pasta.*

*Piedmont*

# BAGNET
### (Bagnet)

———— ❦❦❦ ————

*Bagnet* is a parsley and garlic sauce, not unlike the Ligurian *pesto*. It is indispensable to the Piedmontese household, where it is used more as a condiment than a sauce. Add a teaspoon or two to sauces, soups, vegetable stews, or even salad dressings. Or use it sparingly as a sauce for pasta or stirred into a risotto. *Bagnet* keeps well for up to one week in an airtight jar in the refrigerator.

2    cups roughly chopped fresh parsley
8    to 10 garlic cloves, crushed
1/2  cup olive oil, approximately
     Salt
     Freshly ground black pepper

Place the parsley, garlic, olive oil, and salt and black pepper to taste in a blender and mix slowly until the mixture is smooth. Spoon into an airtight glass jar and pour olive oil over the top to form a quarter-inch thick layer.

*All Italy*

## VINAIGRETTE SAUCE
*(Salsa vinaigrette)*

A good vinaigrette sauce depends on the quality of the oil and vinegar used. Choose a fruity virgin olive oil and a mild wine vinegar. An excellent wine vinegar, *aceto balsamico di Modena,* is becoming more readily available at Italian specialty stores and gourmet shops. This is an herb-flavored wine vinegar that has been made in Modena since the eleventh century. One bottle takes a minimum of 10 years to produce. The result is a remarkably smooth and delicious vinegar. The people of Modena claim it is rich in medicinal qualities.

1/3 cup wine vinegar
1 cup virgin olive oil
2 garlic cloves, crushed
  Few leaves of fresh basil
  Salt
  Freshly ground black pepper

Combine all the ingredients with seasoning to taste in a small glass jar. Screw the cap on firmly and shake well until the vinaigrette sauce is slightly thickened. *Makes 1 1/3 cups.*

*All Italy*

# MAYONNAISE
### (Maionese)

❦ ❦ ❦

To make a good mayonnaise both the egg yolks and the oil should be at room temperature. Beat the oil in very slowly at the beginning. This will help to prevent the yolks from separating. Should this happen, simply start again with a fresh egg yolk and beat in the separated mixture, drop by drop, before adding the remaining oil.

2   egg yolks
2   tablespoons lemon juice, or to taste
    Salt
    Pinch of cayenne pepper
1½  cups olive oil
1   tablespoon boiling water

Place the egg yolks in a mixing bowl with a few drops of lemon juice, and salt and cayenne pepper to taste. Very slowly beat in the oil, drop by drop, with a wire whisk, beating constantly. When the mixture becomes very thick, thin it with a few drops of lemon juice. After the oil is all added, gradually beat in 1 tablespoon boiling water. This will improve the consistency and help to prevent the mayonnaise from separating. *Makes 2 cups.*

*Liguria and the North*

## GREEN MAYONNAISE WITH PISTACHIO NUTS
*(Maionese verde)*

———— 🥖🥖🥖 ————

1 cup homemade Mayonnaise (previous recipe)
1 handful of fresh parsley, chopped
3 or 4 leaves of fresh spinach, shredded
1 teaspoon fresh mint
2 teaspoons pistachio nuts, finely chopped

Place the mayonnaise, parsley, spinach, mint, and pistachio nuts in a blender and blend on high speed until very smooth. *Makes 1 1/2 cups.*

# SOUPS

᪥᪥᪥

## MINESTRE

Italian soups fall into three categories: broths or clear soups, cream soups, and vegetable soups. Broths are usually served with some kind of pasta, which can vary from the tiny *acine di pepe* (peppercorns), to any of the large stuffed ravioli.

Cream soups are usually puréed and thickened with eggs, cream, or béchamel sauce; they are sometimes served with the addition of pasta or croutons.

Vegetable soups also fall into three categories: *zuppa*, which always includes bread, toast; or croutons; *minestra*, a vegetable soup with rice or pasta; and *minestrone*, a bigger or more substantial version of *minestra*. *Minestroni* are often a meal in a soup. Both *minestre* and *minestroni* are always served with grated cheese on the side.

*All Italy*

# VEGETABLE BROTH
*(Brodo)*

Broth plays an integral part in Italian cooking, as it is the foundation of many soups and rice dishes.

2½   quarts water
2   small potatoes
1   leek, thinly sliced
1   onion, chopped
1   small bunch of celery, diced
4   carrots, sliced
2   bay leaves
1   handful of fresh parsley, chopped
⅛   teaspoon dried thyme
1   teaspoon salt
6   peppercorns

Combine all the ingredients in a large pot and bring slowly to a boil. Simmer for 1½ to 2 hours. Strain through a fine sieve. The broth will keep for 2 or 3 days in the refrigerator. *Makes 2 quarts.*

*Calabria*

## POTATO AND ONION SOUP
### *(Licurdia)*

This is a simple potato soup, flavored with onions and hot pepper. A specialty of Cosenza.

1   pound potatoes, diced
1   pound onions, sliced
1/4  head of Boston lettuce, shredded
2   quarts water
3   tablespoons olive oil
1/8  teaspoon hot red pepper flakes
    Salt
6   slices of whole-wheat bread, cut into croutons and dried in a 375°F. oven
1   cup freshly grated pecorino cheese

Bring the potatoes, onions, and lettuce slowly to a boil in 2 quarts of water. Simmer for 45 minutes over very low heat.

Add the olive oil, hot pepper, and salt to taste. Simmer for 5 minutes. Place the croutons in individual soup bowls, pour soup over the croutons, and serve at once with grated cheese on the side. *Serves 6.*

*Veneto*

# CREAM OF CELERY SOUP
## (Crema di sedani)

A specialty of Verona

| | |
|---|---|
| 2 | tablespoons butter |
| 3 | cups thinly sliced celery |
| 1 | large leek, thinly sliced |
| 1 | medium-size potato, diced |
| 1½ | quarts broth or water |
| 1 | egg yolk |
| 1 | cup light cream |
| ¼ | cup freshly grated Parmesan cheese |
| ¼ | teaspoon freshly grated nutmeg |
| | Salt |
| | Freshly ground black pepper |

Heat the butter in a large pot and cook the celery, leek, and potato over moderate heat for 3 minutes. Add the broth and bring to a boil. Cover and simmer for 30 minutes. Force through a sieve or purée in a blender, and return to the pot. Beat the egg yolk, cream, and grated cheese together. Beat ½ cup of hot soup into the egg and cream mixture, then stir the mixture back into the soup. Add the nutmeg, and salt and black pepper to taste. Heat to just below a simmer. Do not boil or the soup will curdle. Serve at once. *Serves 4.*

*Piedmont*

## CREAM OF MUSHROOM SOUP
### *(Crema di funghi)*

2   tablespoons olive oil
1   pound fresh mushrooms, sliced
¼   cup dry Marsala wine
4   cups Béchamel Sauce (page 61)
1   cup Vegetable Broth (page 69), hot
½   cup light cream, heated
    Salt
    Freshly ground black pepper
2   tablespoons finely chopped fresh parsley

Heat the olive oil in a pot and cook the mushrooms over moderate heat for 5 minutes. Add the Marsala; raise the heat and cook until it has almost evaporated. Add the béchamel sauce and 1 cup broth and simmer for 15 minutes. Force through a sieve or purée in a blender. Return to the pot and stir in the hot cream, and salt and black pepper to taste. Heat thoroughly. Sprinkle with parsley and serve at once. *Serves 4.*

*Lombardy*

## CREAM OF ASPARAGUS SOUP
### *(Crema di asparagi)*

1   pound asparagus
1   leek, thinly sliced
2   tablespoons butter

2   medium potatoes, diced
1   quart water
¼   cup single cream
    Salt
    Freshly ground black pepper

Trim the ends of the asparagus and with a sharp knife; remove any fibrous parts from the lower stalks. Cut into 2-inch lengths. Heat the butter in a large pot and cook the asparagus and leek over a moderate heat for 2 minutes. Add the potatoes and 1 quart water. Bring to a boil, cover, and simmer for 30 minutes, or until the vegetables are tender. Force through a sieve or purée in a blender. Return to the pot and stir in the cream. Season with salt and black pepper to taste. Heat thoroughly and serve at once. *Serves 4.*

*Emilia-Romagna*

## SWISS CHARD SOUP
### *(Zuppa di bietole)*

1     large bunch of Swiss chard
1½   quarts Vegetable Broth (page 69) or water
1     egg yolks
½     cup light cream
½     cup freshly grated Parmesan cheese
¼     teaspoon freshly grated nutmeg
       Salt
       Freshly ground black pepper
6     slices of whole-wheat bread, cut into
       croutons and dried in a 375°F. oven

Wash the Swiss chard carefully. Cook in a covered saucepan over moderate heat for 5 minutes. The water clinging to the leaves will be sufficient to prevent scorching. Drain chard and chop it finely. Bring the broth to a boil, add the Swiss chard, and simmer for 5 minutes. Beat egg yolks with the cream and grated cheese. Remove the soup from the heat. Beat ½ cup of the hot soup into the egg-yolk and cream mixture, then stir the mixture into the rest of the soup. Season with nutmeg, salt and black pepper to taste. Gently heat to just below the simmer. Do not boil or the soup will curdle. Serve at once with croutons. *Serves 6.*

*L o m b a r d y*

## PUMPKIN SOUP
*(Minestra di zucca)*

— 🌾🌾🌾 —

This is a delicious velvety smooth soup, with a hint of spice. It may be made with butternut or winter squash when pumpkin is out of season.

        2  tablespoons olive oil
        1  small pumpkin, 1½ to 2 pounds, peeled, seeded, and diced
        3  potatoes, diced
        1  bay leaf
        1  tablespoon parsley
       ¼  teaspoon ground coriander
       ¼  teaspoon freshly grated nutmeg
           Pinch of ground cuminseed
        1  quart Vegetable Broth (page 69) or water
        3  cups milk
        1  teaspoon salt
           Freshly ground black pepper
        2  tablespoons butter

1   cup freshly grated Parmesan cheese

Heat the olive oil in a large pot and cook the pumpkin, potatoes, and herbs over moderate heat for 3 minutes. Add the spices and broth. Bring to a boil, cover, and simmer for 1 hour. Remove the bay leaf. Force soup through a sieve or purée in a blender and return to the pot. Add the milk, salt, and black pepper to taste and bring to a boil. Stir in the butter and serve with grated cheese on the side. *Serves 6.*

*L i g u r i a*

## PREBOGGION
### (Preboggion)

———— ❦❦❦ ————

*Preboggion* are bunches of wild herbs and greens found in the region around Genoa. This delicious soup is rich in vitamins and minerals. Add as many different leafy vegetables and herbs as you have on hand. The soup is thickened with rice and enriched with pesto sauce

2   tablespoons olive oil
1   small onion
1   celery rib, thinly sliced
1   handful of parsley, chopped
1   tablespoon fresh marjoram, or 1/2 teaspoon dried
1   tablespoon snipped fresh chives, or 1 teaspoon dried
1/4   head of Savoy cabbage, shredded
1/4   pound Swiss chard, shredded

¼    pound beet greens, shredded
¼    pound spinach, shredded
1    bunch of watercress, shredded
1½    quarts Vegetable Broth (page 69) or water
1    cup raw rice
     Salt
     Freshly ground black pepper
½    cup Pesto Sauce (page 62)
1    cup freshly grated pecorino sardo or
     Parmesan cheese

Heat the olive oil in a large pot and cook the onion, celery, parsley, marjoram, and chives over moderate heat for 3 minutes. Add the Savoy cabbage, Swiss chard, beet greens, spinach, watercress, and broth. Bring to a boil and simmer for 30 minutes. Increase the heat; when the soup is boiling, add the rice and cook for 20 minutes, or until rice is tender but still firm. Remove from the heat, stir in the pesto sauce, and season with salt and black pepper to taste. Serve at once with grated cheese on the side. *Serves 6.*

*L o m b a r d y*

## R I C E ,  P E A ,  A N D  L E T T U C E  S O U P
*(Minestra di riso, piselle, e lattuga)*

This is a light and refreshing summer soup.

1    tablespoon butter
1    tablespoon olive oil
2    quarts Vegetable Broth (page 69)
1½    cups shelled fresh peas
1    head of Boston lettuce, shredded
1    cup raw rice

Salt
Freshly ground black pepper
1 cup freshly grated Parmesan cheese

Heat the butter and olive oil in a large pot. Add 2 quarts broth and
the peas. Bring to a boil and cook for 20 minutes, or until peas are
tender. Add the shredded lettuce and salt and black pepper to taste
and simmer for 10 minutes. Raise the heat; when soup is boiling,
add the rice, salt, and black pepper. Cook for 20 minutes, or until
rice is tender but still firm. Serve at once, with grated cheese on
the side. *Serves 6.*

*Friuli and Venezia Giulia*

## RICE AND LEMON SOUP
*(Minestra di riso e limone)*

——— 🌿🌿🌿 ———

This refreshing summer soup reveals a Greek
influence.

2 quarts Vegetable Broth (page 69)
1 cup raw rice
4 egg yolks
½ cup freshly grated Parmesan cheese
Juice of ½ lemon

Bring the broth to a boil in a large pot, and pour in the rice. In a
bowl beat the egg yolks with 2 tablespoons of the Parmesan cheese.
Slowly beat in the lemon juice in droplets. When the rice is tender
but still firm, remove from heat. Slowly spoon a ladleful of hot soup
into the egg mixture. Gradually pour the mixture back into the hot
soup. Heat thoroughly. Serve with remaining Parmesan cheese on
the side. *Serves 6.*

*Sicily*

# RICE AND LENTIL SOUP
### *(Minestra di riso e lenticchie)*

This is a warming, substantial soup, rich in protein. Use the small green lentils found in Italian groceries or gourmet shops.

1 cup green lentils
2 quarts water
3 tablespoons olive oil
2 garlic cloves, crushed
1 small onion, chopped
1 cup canned plum tomatoes, seeded and chopped
1/2 cup raw rice
Salt
Freshly ground black pepper
1/2 cup freshly grated pecorino cheese

Wash the lentils carefully and bring to a boil in 1 1/2 quarts water. Cover and simmer for 1 1/2 hours, or until lentils are tender.

Heat the olive oil in a large pot and cook the garlic and onion over moderate heat for 3 minutes. Add the chopped tomatoes and cook over high heat for 5 minutes. Add the lentils and their cooking liquid, salt and black pepper to taste, and enough water to make 2 quarts. Bring to a boil and simmer for 30 minutes. Raise the heat; when the soup is boiling, pour in the rice. Cook for 20 minutes, or until rice is tender but still firm. Serve at once, with grated cheese on the side. *Serves 4.*

*Valle d'Aosta*

# CABBAGE AND FONTINA CHEESE SOUP
*(Zuppa alla valpelleunenze)*

———— 🦪🦪🦪 ————

This is a cross between a soup and a casserole. Layers of bread, cabbage, and fontina cheese are arranged in a large casserole and bathed in broth. The "soup" is then baked in the oven until the cabbage is very tender and the top is nicely browned.

 1   small head of green cabbage
12   slices of French bread, about ¹/₂ inch thick
 6   ounces fontina cheese, thinly sliced
 2   quarts Vegetable Broth (page 69)
³/₄  cup freshly grated Parmesan cheese
 2   ounces butter, melted

Wash the cabbage, discard the tough outer leaves, and cut the head into quarters. Steam for 7 minutes, or until tender. Allow to cool, then chop finely. Place the French bread in a single layer in a large casserole. Cover with chopped cabbage and top with slices of fontina cheese. Pour the hot broth over all and sprinkle with grated cheese. Dribble melted butter over the top. Bake in a preheated 325°F. oven for 1 hour, or until the cabbage is very soft and the top is lightly browned. Serve at once. *Serves 6.*

*Piedmont*

## GARDEN VEGETABLE SOUP
*(Minestra giardiniera)*

This is a simple light vegetable soup using early summer vegetables. No pasta, rice, or bread is used to thicken this soup.

1   tablespoon butter
2   tablespoons olive oil
1   garlic clove, crushed
1   leek, thinly sliced
3   carrots, diced
1   turnip, diced
2   potatoes, peeled and diced
1½   quarts Vegetable Broth (page 69) or water
1   cup shelled fresh peas
1   head of Boston lettuce, shredded
    Salt
    Freshly ground black pepper
1   cup freshly grated Parmesan cheese

Heat the butter and olive oil in a large pot and cook the garlic, leek, carrots, turnip, and potatoes over moderate heat for 5 minutes. Add 1½ quarts of broth, the peas, lettuce, and salt and black pepper to taste. Bring to a boil and simmer for 30 minutes, or until the vegetables are just tender. Serve with grated cheese on the side. *Serves 4.*

*Valle d'Aosta*

## ALPINE SPLIT-PEA SOUP
*(Crema di verdure passati)*

|  |  |
|---|---|
| 1 | cup dried split peas |
| 1½ | quarts Vegetable Broth (page 69) |
| 2 | tablespoons olive oil |
| 1 | large onion, thinly sliced |
| 2 | carrots, diced |
| 1 | turnip, diced |
| 1 | leek, thinly sliced |
| 2 | medium-size potatoes, diced |
| 1 | bay leaf |
| ½ | cup light cream |
| 1 | teaspoon salt |
|  | Freshly ground black pepper |
| 6 | slices of whole-wheat bread, cut into croutons and dried in a 375°F. oven until golden |

Soak the split peas in water overnight and drain.

Bring peas to a boil in 1½ quarts broth and simmer for 1½ hours, or until the peas are tender. Heat the olive oil in a large pot and cook the onion, carrots, turnip, leek, and potatoes over moderate heat for 5 minutes. Add the split peas and their cooking liquid, cover, and simmer for 20 minutes. Remove the bay leaf. Force soup through a sieve or purée in a blender and return to the pot. If the mixture is too thick, thin with a little boiling water. Stir in the cream, salt, and black pepper to taste. Heat thoroughly. Serve with croutons. *Serves 6.*

*Veneto*

# Pasta and Bean Soup
*(Paste e fasioi)*

This is a classic Venetian soup made with the famous white beans from Lamon. Cannellini or small white beans may be used instead. As is the case with many Tuscan bean soups, half of the cooked beans are puréed and used to thicken the soup.

| | |
|---|---|
| 2 | cups dried white beans |
| 1/3 | cup olive oil |
| 2 | garlic cloves, crushed |
| 1 | small onion, chopped |
| 1 | celery rib, thinly sliced |
| 1 | handful of parsley, finely chopped |
| 1 | bay leaf |
| 1/2 | cup canned plum tomatoes, forced through a sieve or puréed in a food processor |
| 2½ | quarts Vegetable Broth (page 69) |
| 1/2 | pound egg noodles |
| 1/2 | cup freshly grated Parmesan cheese |

Soak the beans in water overnight and drain.

Heat the olive oil in a large pot and cook the garlic, onion, celery, parsley, and bay leaf for 2 minutes. Add the tomato purée, drained beans, and 2½ quarts broth. Bring slowly to a boil and cook for 1½ to 2 hours, or until the beans are tender. Remove the bay leaf. Purée half of the beans and vegetables and return to the pot. The soup should have the consistency of thin cream. If it is too thick, thin it with a little water. Bring slowly to a boil and simmer for 5 minutes. Raise the heat; when the soup is boiling, drop in the egg noodles and cook until they are tender but still firm. Serve with grated cheese on the side. *Serves 6.*

*Friuli and Venezia Giulia*

## BEAN AND BARLEY SOUP
*(Minestra di fagioli e orzo)*

1 cup dried white beans
3/4 cup pearl barley
2 quarts water
3 tablespoons olive oil
2 garlic cloves, crushed
1 celery rib, diced
1 carrot, diced
1 small bunch parsley, finely chopped
1/4 teaspoon ground cuminseed
1 bay leaf
1 cup canned plum tomatoes, forced through
   a sieve or puréed in the blender
1/2 cup freshly grated Parmesan cheese
   Salt
   Freshly ground black pepper

Soak the beans in water overnight and drain.

Stir drained beans and barley into 2 quarts of water and bring to a boil. Cover and simmer for 2 hours, or until beans and barley are tender. Heat the olive oil in a large pot and cook the garlic, celery, carrot, parsley, cuminseed, and bay leaf over moderate heat for 3 minutes. Add the tomato purée, the beans and barley and their cooking liquid, and salt and black pepper to taste. Simmer for 30 minutes, or until the celery and carrots are tender. Serve with grated cheese on the side. *Serves 4 to 6.*

*Piedmont*

## Chick-Pea and Turnip Soup
### *(Cisrá)*

|       |                                                    |
|------:|----------------------------------------------------|
| 2     | cups dried chick-peas                              |
| 2½    | quarts water                                       |
| 3     | tablespoons olive oil                              |
| 2     | garlic cloves, crushed                             |
| 1     | small onion, chopped                               |
| 1     | turnip, diced                                      |
| 1     | celery rib, thinly sliced                          |
| ½     | pound turnip tops, shredded                        |
|       | Salt                                               |
|       | Freshly ground black pepper                        |
| 6     | slices of whole-wheat bread, cut into croutons and dried in a 375°F. oven |
| 1     | cup freshly grated Parmesan cheese                 |

Soak the chick-peas in water overnight and drain.

Bring peas to a boil in 2½ quarts water and cook for 2½ to 3 hours, or until chick-peas are tender. Heat the olive oil in a large pot and cook the garlic, onion, turnip, and celery over moderate heat for 8 to 10 minutes, until the vegetables are tender and starting to turn golden. Add the chick-peas and their cooking liquid, the shredded turnip tops, and salt and black pepper to taste. Simmer for 30 minutes more. Place the croutons in individual soup bowls and pour the soup over them. Serve with grated cheese on the side. *Serves 6.*

*Emilia-Romagna*

## ZUCCHINI SOUP
*(Zuppa di zucchini)*

3   tablespoon olive oil
1   small onion, chopped
1   bay leaf
1   handful of parsley, chopped
1   teaspoon fresh basil, or ¼ teaspoon dried
1   pound zucchini, sliced
2   quarts Vegetable Broth (page 69)
2   eggs
1   cup freshly grated Parmesan cheese
6   slices of whole-wheat bread, cut into
    croutons and dried in a 375°F. oven until
    golden

Heat the olive oil in a pot and cook the onion and herbs for 3
minutes. Add the zucchini and hot broth. Bring to a boil, cover, and
simmer for 25 minutes, or until the zucchini are tender. Remove
the bay leaf. Force soup through a food mill or purée in a blender
and return to the pot. In a bowl beat the eggs with half of the grated
cheese. Gradually mix a ladleful of hot soup into the eggs, then
slowly stir the mixture into the rest of the soup. Heat through but
do not boil. Place the croutons in individual soup bowls and pour
the soup over them. Serve with remaining grated cheese on the
side. *Serves 4 to 6.*

*Tuscany*

## TUSCAN MINESTRONE SOUP
### *(Minestrone alla toscana)*

The most important ingredient of Tuscan minestrone soup is the dried beans. Usually all or
part of the cooked beans are puréed before
they are added to the soup. Either rice or
pasta may be used as an additional thickener.

1 cup dried white beans
2 quarts water
3 tablespoons olive oil
2 garlic cloves, crushed
1 small onion, chopped
1 celery rib, thinly sliced
1 leek, thinly sliced
    Pinch of rosemary
    Pinch of thyme
1 handful of parsley, chopped
1 pound kale, shredded
1/2 head of escarole shredded
1 cup canned plum tomatoes, forced through a
    sieve or puréed in a food processor
3/4 cup uncooked elbow macaroni
1 cup freshly grated Parmesan cheese

Soak the dried beans in water overnight and drain.

Bring beans to a boil in 2 quarts water, cover, and simmer for 1 1/2
hours, or until beans are tender. Force the beans and the cooking
liquid through a sieve or purée in a blender. Set aside. Heat the
olive oil in a large pot and cook the garlic, onion, celery, leek, and
herbs over moderate heat for 3 minutes. Add the kale and escarole
and cook for 5 minutes more. Stir in the tomato purée and the bean

purée. Add a little more water if the soup is too thick. Bring slowly to a boil, cover, and simmer for 15 minutes. Raise the heat; when the soup is boiling, drop in the elbow macaroni and cook until it is tender but still firm. *Serves 6.*

*Liguria*

## MINESTRONE SOUP WITH PESTO
### *(Minestrone col pesto)*

The selection of vegetables used in minestrone soup varies from region to region. In Liguria, a typical minestrone soup consists of lima beans, zucchini, green beans, peas, and potatoes. Eggplant and cardoons are sometimes included. What makes a Ligurian minestrone unique is the addition of the famous pesto sauce. Either pasta or rice may be used as an additional thickener.

| | |
|---|---|
| 1/4 | cup olive oil |
| 2 | garlic cloves, crushed |
| 1 | onion, chopped |
| 1 | celery rib, thinly sliced |
| 1 | handful of parsley, chopped |
| 2 | zucchini, diced |
| 1 | cup 1-inch lengths of green beans |
| 1 | cup shelled fresh lima beans |
| 1 | cup shelled fresh peas |
| 2 | potatoes, diced |
| 1/4 | head of Savoy cabbage, shredded |
| 1 | pound Swiss chard, shredded |
| 2 | quarts water |

¹/₂  pound uncooked egg noodles, broken into
      2-inch lengths
1   cup Pesto Sauce (page 62)
1   cup freshly grated Parmesan cheese

Heat the olive oil in a large pot and cook the garlic, onion, celery, and parsley over moderate heat for 3 minutes. Add the zucchini, green beans, lima beans, peas, potatoes, cabbage, Swiss chard, and 2 quarts water. Bring to a boil, cover, and simmer for 1¹/₂ hours. Raise the heat; when the soup is boiling, drop in the egg noodles and cook until tender but still firm. Remove from the heat. Stir in the pesto sauce and serve at once with grated cheese on the side. *Serves 6.*

*A p u l i a*

### Green Minestrone
*(Minestrone verde alla barese)*

A specialty of Bari. The green vegetables may be varied according to what is in season. Cabbage, spinach, kale, beet greens, watercress, and escarole all make excellent variations.

3   tablespoons olive oil
2   garlic cloves, crushed
1   onion, chopped
1   fennel bulb, diced
2   celery ribs, thinly sliced
1   pound potatoes, diced
1   pound Swiss chard, shredded
¹/₂  pound collards, shredded
¹/₂  pound beet greens, shredded

  ¹/₂  pound turnip tops, shredded
  2  quarts Vegetable Broth or water
  1  bay leaf
     Pinch of ground cloves
     Salt
     Freshly ground black pepper
  ³/₄  cup uncooked short macaroni, ¹/₄ to ¹/₂
     inch in length
  1  cup freshly grated Parmesan cheese

Heat the olive oil in a large pot and cook the garlic, onion, fennel, and celery over moderate heat for 5 minutes. Add the potatoes, Swiss chard, collards, beet greens, and turnip tops and continue to cook for 5 minutes. Add 2 quarts of water, the bay leaf, cloves, and salt and black pepper to taste. Bring to a boil, cover, and simmer for 1 hour. Increase the heat; when the soup is boiling, add the macaroni and cook until it is tender but still firm. Serve with grated cheese on the side. *Serves 6.*

*Calabria*

## MILLECOSEDDE
*(Millecosedde)*

—— 🌿🌿🌿 ——

*Millecosedde* means "a thousand little things."
All the odds and ends of pasta, dried beans,
and vegetables can be used up in this recipe.

  ¹/₂  cup dried white beans
  ¹/₂  cup dried chick-peas
  ¹/₂  cup dried green lentils
  2¹/₂  quarts water
  3  tablespoons olive oil

2   garlic cloves, crushed
1   onion, chopped
1   carrot, diced
2   celery ribs, thinly sliced
1   turnip, diced
1   potato, diced
1   handful of parsley, chopped
1   teaspoon fresh oregano, or $1/4$ teaspoon
    dried
1   bay leaf
$1/4$   pound mushrooms, sliced
1   pound beet greens or spinach, shredded
1   pound collards, shredded
    Salt
    Freshly ground black pepper
$1/3$   pound uncooked short macaroni or
    spaghetti, broken into 2-inch lengths
1   cup freshly grated pecorino cheese

Soak the dried vegetables in water overnight and drain.

Bring to a boil in $2^{1/2}$ quarts water and simmer, covered, for 2 hours, or until all the dried vegetables are tender. Pour off and reserve the cooking liquid.

Heat the olive oil in a large pot and cook the garlic, onion, carrot, celery, turnip, potato, parsley, and oregano over moderate heat for 5 minutes. Add the bay leaf, mushrooms, beet greens, and collards and cook for 5 minutes more. Add the reserved cooking liquid, and salt and black pepper to taste. Bring to a boil and simmer for 1 hour. Add the drained dried vegetables and a little more water if the soup is too thick. Raise the heat; when the soup is boiling, add the pasta and cook until it is tender but still firm. Serve with grated cheese on the side. *Serves 6.*

# *GRAINS*

## *Bread*
### *(Pane)*

Bread is still the staff of life in Italy, especially in the poorer regions of the South. Although most Americans think of Italian bread as white and crusty, similar to French bread, darker more solid bread can be found.

In this chapter you will find recipes for two of these darker, more nutritious loaves. One is a firm, close-grained barley bread from Lombardy, the other is *pane integrale,* a lighter, softer whole-meal bread that is made all over Italy.

### *Lombardy*

## BARLEY BREAD
### *(Brazadel)*

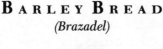

*Brazadel* is a delicious crusty barley bread found in the Valtellina Valley. The grain is coarse and grayish. The bread keeps very well.

1½   packages (4½ teaspoons) active dry yeast

2  cups warm water (105–115°F.)
2  tablespoons honey
2  cups barley flour
2  cups whole-wheat flour
2  cups unbleached white flour
2  tablespoons olive oil
2  teaspoons salt

Dissolve the yeast in the warm water in a large mixing bowl. Stir in the honey and leave for 5 minutes until the yeast is foamy. Place the barley, whole-wheat, and unbleached white flour in a bowl and blend well together. Add half of the flour mixture to the yeast and beat together with a wooden spoon for 10 minutes to incorporate plenty of air in the dough, which should have the consistency of thick mud. Cover with plastic wrap and leave in a warm place for 1 hour until the dough has doubled in bulk.

Punch the dough down and carefully fold in the olive oil and salt and ½ cup flour. Gradually fold in more flour until the dough starts to come away from the sides of the bowl. Place the dough on a lightly floured work surface and knead well for 10 minutes. Add more flour as necessary. Place the dough in a lightly oiled mixing bowl. Cover with plastic wrap and leave in a warm place until the dough has doubled in bulk. (If you are in a hurry you may omit the second rising, but the bread will be a little heavier.)

Punch the dough down. Place on a lightly floured work surface and shape into 2 domed round loaves. Cut a cross in the center of each loaf. Place on an oiled baking sheet and cover with a kitchen towel. Let rise until doubled in bulk, about 45 minutes to 1 hour. Bake in a preheated 350°F. oven for about 50 minutes. When the bread is done it will sound slightly hollow when tapped. Cool thoroughly on a wire rack before eating. *Makes 2 Loaves.*

*All Italy*

## WHOLE-MEAL BREAD
*(Pane integrale)*

*Pane integrale* or whole-meal bread is found in most regions of Italy. Whole-wheat flour is combined with white flour to make a softer, lighter loaf than the usual whole-wheat bread.

   2   packages active dry yeast
   3   cups warm water (105°F.–115°F.)
   3   tablespoons honey
   5   cups whole-wheat flour
2¹⁄₂   cups unbleached white flour
   2   teaspoons salt
   2   tablespoons olive oil

Follow the same directions as for Barley Bread (previous recipe). After the second rising, punch the dough down. Place on a lightly floured work surface and shape into 2 domed round loaves. Cut a cross in the center of each loaf. Place loaves on an oiled baking sheet. Bake in a preheated 350°F. oven for about 50 minutes. When the bread is done it will sound slightly hollow when tapped. Cool thoroughly on a wire rack before eating. *Makes 2 loaves.*

## Flat Bread
*(Focaccia)*

*Focaccia,* or flat bread, is a descendant of the ancient hearth cake that the Romans introduced around Europe. The dough was baked on hearthstones under the ashes of the fire, producing ashcakes or *focaccie.*

   *Focaccia* is primarily made in northern Italy and is the forerunner of the pizza that is made in the South. Today, *focaccie* are leavened with yeast and baked in the oven. There are many versions of this flat bread. Some are flavored very simply with rosemary or sage, some are studded with olives, others are topped with onions or sun-dried tomatoes.

*Focaccie* are easy to make. The exact thickness of the dough depends on your preference. They may be made ½ inch thick, which produces a crisp, crackerlike crust, or they may be made up to 2 inches thick, which is more like a bread.

*E m i l i a - R o m a g n a*

## F L A T  B R E A D  W I T H  O L I V E S
*(Focaccia con olive)*

        1    package active dry yeast
        1    cup warm water (105°–115°F.)
      3⅓    to 4 cups whole-wheat or unbleached
               white flour
        5    tablespoons olive oil
       ¾    cup black Italian or Greek olives, pitted
               and sliced
        1    teaspoon salt
               Cornmeal

Stir the yeast into the warm water in a large mixing bowl. Let stand for 10 minutes until the yeast is dissolved and the mixture is light beige and creamy. Stir in 2 cups of the flour and beat until the dough forms a sticky mass. Sprinkle some of the remaining flour on a work surface or large board and turn out the sticky dough on the board. Gradually knead in remaining flour until the dough is smooth and elastic and no longer sticks to your hands. Place in an oiled bowl, cover, and let rise in a warm place for 1 hour, until the dough has doubled in bulk.

Punch the dough down carefully and fold in 4 tablespoons olive oil, the sliced olives, and salt. Place on the floured work surface and knead again until smooth. Roll the dough out to a circle about 10 to 12 inches in diameter. Place on a well-oiled 15-inch pizza pan that has been dusted with cornmeal. Brush the top of the *focaccia* with the remaining tablespoon of olive oil. Let dough rise in the pan for 1 hour, or until doubled in bulk. Bake in a preheated 400°F. oven for 30 minutes, or until the top is golden. For a thinner more crisp *focaccia,* roll out to a 15-inch circle and bake for 20 minutes. *Makes 1 flat loaf.*

*Lombardy*

## Onion Focaccia
### *(Focaccia con cipolle)*

❦❦❦

| | |
|---|---|
| 1 | package active dry yeast |
| 1 | cup warm water (105°–115°F.) |
| 3½ | to 4 cups whole-wheat or unbleached white flour |
| 6 | tablespoons olive oil |
| 1 | teaspoon salt |
| 1 | pound Bermuda onions, thinly sliced |
| | Freshly ground black pepper |
| | Cornmeal |

Follow the directions for Flat Bread with Olives (preceding recipe). After the dough has doubled in bulk, punch down and carefully fold in 4 tablespoons olive oil and the salt. Place on the work surface and knead again until smooth. Roll the dough out to a circle about 10 to 12 inches in diameter, or you may flatten the dough into shape with your hands. Any indentations on the surface will help to hold the topping. Place the focaccia on a well-oiled 15-inch pizza pan that has been dusted with cornmeal. Let rise for 1 hour.

Heat remaining olive oil in a frying pan and gently cook the onions for 8 to 10 minutes, or until they are translucent. Spread onions over the risen dough and sprinkle with black pepper. Bake in a pre-heated 425°F. oven for 30 minutes, or until the bread is golden. *Makes 1 flat loaf.*

## Pizza, Calzone, and Panzarotti
### (Pizza, Calzone, E Panzarotti)

"Bread with a relish" was a favorite snack of both the Romans and the ancient Greeks. The relish might consist of olive oil, herbs, wine, spices, olives, or cheese. It was the Greeks who first started baking the relish together with the bread and so created the fore-runner of pizza as we know it today.

The Neapolitans transformed this poor man's dish into a medley of bread, vegetables, herbs, and cheese. The tomato was intro-duced into Neapolitan cooking in the eighteenth century, but it was not until 1889 that the classic pizza of tomatoes, cheese, olive oil, and herbs was invented, in commemoration of the Italian flag, and named in honor of Queen Margherita, who was an avid pizza lover.

Pizza literally means "pie." Many versions of pizza are found all over Italy. Some are double-crust pies, like *pizza alla perugina*, which has a simple filling of Gruyère cheese. Others are more like a bread, such as the cheese-flavored *pizza di formaggio* from Ancona.

Another favorite form of pizza is the *calzone*, which literally means "trouser leg." It is, simply, a folded pizza that has been stuffed with pizza topping, then baked in the oven, or possibly deep-fried.

*Panzerotti* is an even smaller relative of *calzone*. It is a stuffed turnover, 2 to 3 inches long, made of pastry or pasta dough, then baked in the oven or deep-fried until crisp and golden.

### PIZZA DOUGH

1   package active dry yeast

    1   cup warm water (105°–115°F.)
    3   cups whole-wheat or unbleached white
        flour
  $^1\!/_2$  teaspoon salt

Mix the yeast with the warm water in a large mixing bowl. Let it stand for 10 minutes until the yeast is dissolved and is light beige and creamy. Fold in 2 cups of the flour and beat until the dough forms a sticky mass. Sprinkle some of the remaining flour on a work surface or large board and turn out the sticky dough on it. Gradually knead in remaining flour and the salt, until the dough is smooth and elastic and no longer sticks to your hands. Cover with plastic wrap and let rise in a warm place for about 1 hour, or until doubled in bulk.

Punch the dough down and place again on the floured work surface. Knead briefly. Roll out into a 15-inch circle, no more than $^1\!/_4$ inch thick. Place on a well-oiled pizza pan and top with the topping of your choice. *Makes enough dough for 1 pizza.*

*Campania*

# PIZZA MARGHERITA
### (Pizza Margherita)

This is a classic pizza with a topping of mozzarella cheese, olive oil, and herbs. Canned tomatoes may be used instead of fresh tomatoes.

    1   recipe Pizza Dough (preceding recipe)
       Cornmeal

    1   cup peeled, seeded, and chopped ripe
        plum tomatoes
    3   tablespoons olive oil
    2   teaspoons fresh basil, or $^1/_2$ teaspoon dried
    1   teaspoon fresh oregano, or $^1/_4$ teaspoon
        dried
  $^1/_2$  pound mozzarella cheese, shredded

Roll out the pizza dough to a circle 15 inches in diameter. Place on a well-oiled pizza pan that has been dusted with cornmeal. Let rise in a warm place for 1 hour, until the dough has doubled in bulk.

Drain the chopped tomatoes. Heat 1 tablespoon of olive oil in a frying pan and cook the tomatoes over moderate heat for 5 minutes. Spread over the pizza. Sprinkle with basil and oregano and top with shredded mozzarella cheese. Dribble remaining olive oil over the top. Bake in a preheated 450°F. oven for 15 to 20 minutes. *Serves 4.*

*Campania*

## Pizza with Mushrooms
*(Pizza con funghi)*

    1   recipe Pizza Dough (page 96)
        Cornmeal
    4   tablespoons olive oil
    1   cup canned plum tomatoes
    1   garlic clove, crushed
    2   tablespoons finely chopped parsley
    1   teaspoon fresh oregano, or $^1/_2$ teaspoon
        dried
    1   pound mushrooms, sliced
    6   ounces mozzarella cheese, shredded

3   tablespoons freshly grated Parmesan
cheese

Roll out the pizza dough to a circle 15 inches in diameter. Place on
a well-oiled pizza pan that has been dusted with cornmeal. Let rise
in a warm place for 1 hour, or until doubled in bulk.

Heat 1 tablespoon of olive oil in a frying pan and cook the tomatoes
over moderate heat for 5 minutes. Spread over the pizza. Heat 1
tablespoon of olive oil in another frying pan and cook the garlic,
parsley, and oregano for 1 minute. Add the mushrooms and cook
over moderate heat for 5 minutes, or until they are tender. Spoon
the mushrooms over the tomatoes. Top with mozzarella cheese
and sprinkle with Parmesan cheese. Dribble remaining olive oil
over the top. Bake in a preheated 450°F. oven for 15 to 20 minutes.
*Serves 4.*

*A p u l i a*

# Swiss Chard Pizza
*(Pizza di bietole)*

———— 🦪🦪🦪 ————

1   recipe Pizza Dough (page 96)
Cornmeal
2   pounds Swiss chard
2   tablespoons olive oil
2   garlic cloves, crushed
¹/₂   pound mozzarella cheese, shredded
3   tablespoons freshly grated pecorino cheese
¾   cup black Italian or Greek olives, pitted

Roll out the pizza dough to a circle 15 inches in diameter. Place on
a well-oiled pizza pan that has been dusted with cornmeal. Let rise
in a warm place for 1 hour, or until it has doubled in bulk.

Wash the Swiss chard, cut away the thick ribs, and chop leaves coarsely. Heat the olive oil in a saucepan and cook the garlic for 1 minute. Add the Swiss chard, cover, and cook over moderate heat for 5 minutes, or until chard is tender, stirring constantly, so the leaves cook evenly. Spread the Swiss chard over the pizza. Top with mozzarella cheese, sprinkle with pecorino cheese, and garnish with black olives. Bake in a preheated 450°F. oven for 15 to 20 minutes. *Serves 4.*

*Sicily*

## PIZZA WITH EGGPLANT
*(Pizza alla siciliana)*

———— 🌿🌿🌿 ————

1   recipe Pizza Dough (page 96)
    Cornmeal
1   small eggplant, about ½ pound
    Salt
⅓   cup olive oil
1   cup Tomato Sauce (page 57)
    Pinch of hot red pepper flakes
6   ounces caciocavallo or mozzarella cheese,
    shredded
15  black Italian or Greek black olives
1   tablespoon capers
3   tablespoons freshly grated pecorino cheese

Roll out the pizza dough to a circle 15 inches in diameter. Place on a well-oiled pizza pan that has been dusted with cornmeal. Let rise in a warm place for 1 hour or until it has doubled in bulk.

Peel the eggplant and cut into slices about ⅛ inch thick. Sprinkle with salt and set in a colander for 1 hour to release the bitter juices. Wash off the salt and pat slices dry.

Heat ¼ cup olive oil in a frying pan and quickly brown the eggplant on both sides. Drain on paper towels. Prepare the tomato sauce and add the hot red pepper flakes. Spread sauce over the dough. Cover with the fried eggplant slices. Top with caciocavallo cheese and dot with black olives and capers. Sprinkle the pecorino cheese liberally over the top. Dribble remaining olive oil over all. Bake in a preheated 450°F. oven for 15 to 20 minutes. *Serves 4.*

*Calabria*

# ONION PIE
*(Pitta calabrese)*

In Calabria a stuffed pizza or pie is called a *pitta*. It is an Arab word; the dish dates back to the days when much of southern Italy was overrun by the Saracens.

3 tablespoons olive oil
2 pounds onions, thinly sliced
1 teaspoon fresh oregano
   Salt
   Freshly ground black pepper
1 recipe Pizza Dough (page 96)
   Cornmeal
¼ pound caciocavallo or mozzarella cheese, shredded
¼ cup freshly grated pecorino cheese

Heat the olive oil in a large frying pan and cook the onions and oregano over low heat for 25 to 30 minutes, or until onions are very soft. Do not brown. Sprinkle with salt and black pepper.

Divide the dough in two, making one half larger than the other. Roll out the larger piece into a thin 16-inch circle and arrange on the bottom of a well-oiled 15-inch pizza pan, which has been dusted with cornmeal. Spread the onions over the dough. Cover with caciocavallo cheese and sprinkle with pecorino cheese.

Roll out the second half of dough into a 14-inch circle and place over the filling. Fold the bottom rim over the top edge and press the two layers of dough with a fork, to seal the filling in all around the *pitta*. Brush the top with a little additional olive oil. Bake in a preheated 400°F. oven for 30 to 40 minutes, or until the top is golden. *Serves 4.*

*U m b r i a*

## CHEESE PIE
### *(Pizza alla perugina)*

This is a double-crust pizza with a simple filling of Gruyère cheese. Melted butter and milk are added to the dough to make a softer, richer crust than the usual pizza dough.

    1   package active dry yeast
    1   cup warm milk (105°–115°F.)
    4   cups unbleached white flour
    ⅓   cup melted butter
    ½   teaspoon salt
    ½   pound Gruyère cheese, thinly sliced
    1   egg yolk
    2   tablespoons water

Mix the yeast with the warm milk in a large mixing bowl. Let stand for 10 minutes, until the yeast is dissolved and the mixture is light beige and creamy. Fold in 2 cups of flour and beat until the dough forms a sticky mass. Sprinkle some of the remaining flour on a work surface or large board and turn out the sticky dough on it. Gradually knead in the remaining flour until the dough is smooth and elastic. Place in an oiled bowl and cover with plastic wrap. Let rise in a warm place for 50 to 60 minutes, or until the dough has doubled in bulk.

Punch the dough down and carefully fold in the melted butter and salt. Place on a floured work surface and knead again until smooth. Divide the dough into 2 parts, making one half slightly larger than the other. Roll out the larger half to a circle 14 inches in diameter and arrange over the bottom of a well-oiled pizza pan. Cover with slices of Gruyère cheese, leaving a 2-inch border all around. Roll out the second half of dough to a 12-inch circle and place over the cheese filling. Fold the bottom rim over the top edge and press the two layers of dough with a fork, to seal in the filling. Brush the top lightly with the egg yolk mixed with 2 tablespoons water. Bake in a preheated 400°F. oven for 30 to 40 minutes, or until the top is golden. *Serves 4.*

*L e   M a r c h e*

## CHEESE BREAD
*(Pizza con formaggio all'anconetana)*

A specialty of Ancona

1    package active dry yeast
1    cup warm water (105°–115°F.)
3    cups unbleached white flour,
     approximately
2    eggs
2    tablespoons olive oil

$^1/_2$  cup freshly grated pecorino cheese
3  ounces Gruyère cheese, cut into small dice
$^1/_2$  teaspoon salt

Dissolve the yeast in the warm water in a large mixing bowl. Let stand for 10 minutes until the yeast is dissolved and the mixture is light and creamy. Fold in 2 cups of the flour and beat until the dough forms a sticky mass. Cover with plastic wrap and let dough rise in a warm place for 1 hour, or until it has doubled in bulk.

Beat together the eggs, olive oil, the cheeses, and salt and beat into the raised dough. Sprinkle some of the remaining flour onto a work surface or large board and turn the dough out on it. Gradually knead in remaining flour until the dough is smooth and elastic and no longer sticks to your hands. Place in a well-oiled loaf pan. Cover with plastic wrap and let rise in a warm place for 1$^1/_2$ hours, or until doubled in bulk.

Bake in a preheated 400°F. oven for 35 to 45 minutes, or until the top is golden. *Makes 1 loaf.*

*Campania*

## CALZONI WITH THREE CHEESES
*(Calzoni a tre formaggii)*

1  recipe Pizza Dough (page 96)
1$^1/_2$  cups ricotta cheese
1  whole egg plus 1 extra egg yolk
$^1/_2$  pound mozzarella cheese, cut into small dice
$^1/_2$  cup freshly grated Parmesan cheese
Salt
Freshly ground black pepper

1   egg, beaten with 1 tablespoon water

Divide the dough into 6 pieces and roll out each piece into a circle
8 inches in diameter. In a bowl combine the ricotta cheese, whole
egg, egg yolk, mozzarella and Parmesan cheeses, and salt and black
pepper to taste and blend well. Spoon about ½ cup of filling onto
the lower half of each circle. Brush the edges of the calzone with
the beaten egg. Fold over and crimp the edges securely together
with a fork or your finger. With a spatula carefully transfer the
calzoni to a well-oiled baking sheet. Brush the tops with remaining
beaten egg. Let dough rise in a warm place for 30 minutes.

Bake in a preheated 450°F. oven for 20 to 30 minutes, or until the
tops of the calzoni are golden. *Serves 6.*

*A p u l i a*

## VEGETABLE CALZONI
### (Calzoni con verdure alla barese)

A specialty of Bari, this calzone has a deliciously piquant filling, typical of Apulian cooking.

    1   recipe Pizza Dough (page 96)
    1   head of escarole, about 2 pounds
    3   tablespoons olive oil
    1   small onion, finely chopped
    1   leek, thinly sliced
    1   fennel bulb, cut into small dice
   12   Italian or Greek black olives, pitted and
        sliced
    1   tablespoon capers, roughly chopped

Salt
Freshly ground black pepper
1   egg, beaten with 1 tablespoon water

Divide the dough into 6 pieces and roll out each piece into a circle 8 inches in diameter. Wash the escarole and coarsely shred it. Place in a covered saucepan and cook over moderate heat for 5 minutes, or until it is tender. The water clinging to the leaves is sufficient to prevent scorching. Drain and squeeze dry. Heat the olive oil in a large frying pan and cook the onion, leek, and fennel over moderate heat for 7 minutes, or until the fennel is just tender. Add the escarole, olives, caper, and salt and black pepper to taste. Stir well and simmer for 5 minutes to blend the flavors. Raise the heat at the end to evaporate any liquid.

Spoon ½ cup of the filling onto the lower half of each circle of dough. Brush the edges of the dough with the beaten egg. Fold over and crimp the edges together with a fork or your finger. With a spatula carefully transfer the calzoni to a well-oiled baking sheet. Brush the tops with the remaining beaten egg. Bake in a preheated 450°F. oven for 20 to 30 minutes, or until the tops of the calzoni are golden. May be served hot or at room temperature. *Serves 6.*

*A p u l i a*

# CHEESE PANZAROTTI
### *(Panzarotti con uova e mozzarella)*

These delicious little cheese-filled pastries can be deep-fried or baked in the oven. They are found in Basilicata and Campania as well as Apulia.

 1   recipe Egg Pasta (page 109)
10   ounces mozzarella cheese, shredded
⅓   cup freshly grated Parmesan cheese
 3   eggs
 2   tablespoons finely chopped parsley
     Salt
     Freshly ground black pepper
 2   tablespoon water
     Oil for deep-frying

Follow the directions for egg pasta. Let the dough rest for 30 minutes. In a bowl combine the mozzarella and Parmesan cheeses, 2 eggs, the parsley, and salt and black pepper to taste, and mix well together. Divide the dough into 2 parts and roll out into 2 thin sheets. Place scant teaspoons of the filling over one sheet of the dough at regular intervals about 1½ inches apart. Brush the other sheet of dough with the remaining egg, beaten with 2 tablespoons of water. Place over the first sheet of dough and press well around each mound. With a pastry or ravioli cutter cut the *panzarotti* into 1½-inch squares. Deep-fry in hot oil until crisp and golden on both sides. Drain on paper towels and serve at once.

If you prefer, the *panzarotti* may be brushed lightly with beaten egg or olive oil and baked in a preheated 450°F. oven for 15 minutes. *Serves 4 to 6.*


## Pasta
   *(Pasta)*

Pasta falls into 4 categories. *Pasta secca* is a dry factory-made pasta consisting of flour and water. Contrary to most people's belief, commercial pasta is not a devitalized food, especially when it is made from 100 percent durum semolina. This has had only the bran removed and still contains most of the germ of the wheat. *Pasta all'uovo* is fresh homemade pasta enriched with eggs. The proportion is roughly 1 egg to 1 cup of flour, but this varies slightly

from region to region. Milanese pasta uses 1 egg plus 1 egg yolk to
1 cup of flour. If more than 1¹/₈ cups of flour is used per egg, the
dough will become dry and hard to handle. *Pasta ripiena* is stuffed
pasta, usually homemade but sometimes made of dried pasta. *Pasta
al forno* is baked pasta, which is usually, but not always, made of
dried pasta.

## TO COOK PASTA

Use a minimum of 4 quarts of water to 1 pound of pasta. Add 1
slightly heaped tablespoon of salt and 1 tablespoon of olive oil to
keep the pasta from sticking together. Bring the water to a boil and
keep at a rolling boil throughout cooking. Always stir with a
wooden spoon because this helps to separate the strands of pasta.

The only way to test pasta to see if it is cooked is to taste it. It
should be cooked *al dente,* which means still firm to the bite. Do
not overcook; nothing is worse than a bowl of mushy pasta.

Drain the cooked pasta in a colander or sieve and shake out any
excess moisture. The pasta may be transferred to a heated serving
bowl and tossed with sauce, or it may be heaped directly into individual soup bowls and topped with sauce. This is usually how it is
served in Italy.

## SAUCE

As a general rule, the finer pastas are served with delicate sauces
and the heavier pastas with more substantial sauces.

## CHEESE

However perfectly you prepare the pasta and sauce, if you serve it
with inferior cheese, the result will be inferior. Always buy a fresh
hunk of cheese and grate it just before using. Parmesan, pecorino
sardo, pecorino romano, and asiago are all excellent cheeses for
grating.

## PROPORTIONS FOR PASTA DOUGH

| 3 eggs | 4 eggs | 5 eggs |
|---|---|---|
| 2 cups flour | 2²/₃ cups flour | 3¹/₃ cups flour |
| ¹/₂ teaspoon salt | ¹/₂ teaspoon salt | 1 teaspoon salt |

## WIDTHS OF PASTA

| Tagliarini | ¹/₈ inch wide |
|---|---|
| Fettuccine or Tagliatelle | ¹/₄ inch wide |
| Trenette | ¹/₂ inch wide |
| Pappardelle | ³/₄ inch wide |
| Lasagne | 2 inches wide by 6 inches long |

*E m i l i a - R o m a g n a*

## EGG PASTA
### (La Sfoglia)

Fresh egg pasta is usually made with semolina flour or unbleached plain white flour, or a combination of both. If you prefer, you can use a mixture of whole wheat and plain white flour.

> 2 cups semolina flour or unbleached white flour
> 3 eggs
> ¹/₂ teaspoon salt

Place the flour on a large wooden board on the table. Make a mound of the flour and form a deep well in the center. Drop in 1 egg at a time and add the salt. With a fork gradually beat the flour into the eggs, then form the mixture into a soft ball. Knead the dough well for 8 to 10 minutes, until it is smooth and elastic. Do not add too much flour or the dough will become hard to roll. If the dough is too dry, add a teaspoon or so of water. Wrap the dough in a damp cloth and let it rest for 30 minutes.

Divide dough into 4 portions. Keep 3 parts of the dough wrapped. With a long thin rolling pin, roll out the remaining quarter of dough quickly, making quarter turns to form a circle. Speed is important as the dough will cease to be pliable as it dries out. When the dough is very thin and even, let it dry for 15 to 20 minutes. This will keep the dough from sticking when it is rolled up and cut into noodles of the desired width.

Continue with remaining portions of dough, keeping the pieces wrapped until ready to be rolled.

*Emilia-Romagna*

## SPINACH PASTA
*(Pasta verde)*

*Pasta verde,* or green pasta, can be made equally well with spinach, Swiss chard, or beet greens. In some regions of Italy nettles or mint are included. In Liguria, green pasta is often made with borage instead of spinach.

| | |
|---|---|
| ½ | **pound spinach** |
| 2⅔ | **cups flour** |
| 2 | **eggs** |
| ½ | **teaspoon salt** |

Wash the spinach and cook in a covered saucepan for 5 minutes, until it is tender. The water clinging to the leaves is sufficient to prevent scorching. Squeeze dry and chop very fine.

Place the flour on a large wooden board or table. Make a mound of the flour and form a deep well in the center. Drop in 1 egg at a time, then the spinach and salt. With a fork gradually beat the flour into the eggs. Knead well for 8 to 10 minutes. Proceed as for Egg Pasta (previous recipe).

*Lombardy*

# SAFFRON PASTA WITH ONION SAUCE
### (La rechta con salsa di cipolle)

Milanese pasta dough contains more egg yolks than the dough made in any other region of Italy.

| | | |
|---|---|---|
| *Dough:* | 2 | cups flour |
| | 2 | whole eggs plus 2 egg yolks |
| | 1/2 | teaspoon salt |
| | 1 | teaspoon powdered saffron |

| | | |
|---|---|---|
| *Sauce:* | 3 | tablespoons butter |
| | 2 | tablespoons olive oil |
| | 3 | Spanish onions |
| | 2 | tablespoons finely chopped fresh parsley |
| | 1/2 | cup canned plum tomatoes, forced through a sieve or puréed in a food processor |
| | | Salt |
| | | Freshly ground black pepper |
| | 1 | cup freshly grated Parmesan cheese |

Follow the directions for Egg Pasta on page 109, using 2 whole eggs plus 2 yolks instead of 3 eggs. Beat the saffron with the eggs before mixing them with the flour. While the dough is resting prepare the sauce.

Heat 1 tablespoon of butter and the olive oil in a large frying pan and cook the onions and parsley over low heat for 30 minutes, or until they are almost reduced to a purée. Do not brown. Add the tomato purée and cook over moderate heat for 5 minutes, or until the sauce is thickened. Season with salt and pepper to taste.

Roll out the dough into 2 very thin sheets and let it dry for 10 minutes. If the dough is too moist it will stick to itself when it is rolled out to be cut. Fold each sheet back and forth over itself 3 or 4 times. Cut into noodles ¼ inch thick. Cook the noodles in plenty of lightly salted boiling water until tender but still firm. Transfer to a heated serving bowl, and dot with remaining 2 tablespoons butter. Pour the sauce over the noodles. Toss lightly and serve at once, with grated cheese on the side. *Serves 4.*

*L i g u r i a*

## TRENETTE WITH PESTO SAUCE
*(Trenette col pesto)*

*Trenette* are fresh egg noodles cut into lengths ½ inch wide. The noodles are cooked together with potatoes and green beans, then dressed with pesto sauce.

| *Dough:* | 2 | cups flour |
|---|---|---|
| | 3 | eggs |
| | ½ | teaspoon salt |

*Sauce:*  ½  cup fresh basil
          2  garlic cloves, crushed
          2  tablespoons olive oil
          1  tablespoon pine nuts
          2  tablespoons freshly grated pecorino sardo
             cheese
          2  medium-size potatoes, peeled and diced
          ½  pound green beans, cut into 2-inch lengths
          2  tablespoons butter

Follow the directions for Egg Pasta on page 109. Roll out the dough very thinly and leave to dry for 15 minutes. Roll up and cut into ½-inch-wide noodles. Unfold the *trenette* and spread them out on a large towel or cloth to dry.

Place the basil, garlic, olive oil, and pine nuts in a blender and mix slowly until the ingredients are chopped. Add 1 or 2 tablespoons of hot water and the grated cheese. Blend at high speed until the mixture is smooth and creamy. Cook the potatoes and green beans in a large pot of lightly salted boiling water. When they are almost cooked, add the *trenette* and cook for 5 minutes, or until noodles are tender but still firm. Drain and transfer to a heated serving bowl. Dot with the butter and pour the sauce over all. Toss well and serve at once. *Serves 4.*

*E m i l i a - R o m a g n a*

## TORTELLI WITH SWISS CHARD AND RICOTTA STUFFING
### *(Tortelli d'erbette)*

*Filling:*  1  pound Swiss chard
            1  cup ricotta cheese
            1  egg

        ¹/₂  cup freshly grated Parmesan cheese
           Salt
           Freshly ground black pepper
        ¹/₄  teaspoon freshly grated nutmeg

*Dough:*   2  cups flour
           3  eggs
       ¹/₂  teaspoon salt

*Sauce:*   2  tablespoons butter
       ³/₄  cup heavy cream, brought to the boil
       ³/₄  cup freshly grated Parmesan cheese

Wash the Swiss chard and cook in a covered saucepan over moderate heat for 5 minutes. The water clinging to the leaves is sufficient to prevent scorching. Squeeze dry and roughly chop. In a mixing bowl combine the ricotta cheese, egg, ¹/₂ cup Parmesan cheese, salt and black pepper to taste, and the nutmeg, and blend well.

Follow directions for Egg Pasta on page 109. Let the dough rest and roll it out very thinly. Cut into rounds about 2 inches in diameter. Place a scant teaspoon of filling in the center of each round. Fold over the dough, forming a half circle. Pick up the half circles and bend them around your index finger. Press the two ends well together to form a ring. *Tortelli* are said to resemble the navel of Venus, which is a good guide to their finished shape. Line up the *tortelli* on a lightly floured board or tray and leave for 15 minutes to dry.

Cook the *tortelli* in plenty of lightly salted, boiling water for 5 to 6 minutes. Drain, and transfer to a heated serving dish. Dot with the butter and top with the hot cream and ³/₄ cup grated cheese. Toss lightly and serve at once. *Serves 4.*

*Liguria and the North*

# GREEN RAVIOLI WITH 3 CHEESES
*(Ravioli verde a tre formaggii)*

*Dough:*    2⅔  cups flour
             2  eggs
            ½  pound spinach
            ½  teaspoon salt


*Filling:*   1½  cups ricotta cheese
             1  egg
            ½  cup small dice of mozzarella cheese
            ½  cup freshly grated Parmesan cheese
            ¼  teaspoon freshly grated nutmeg
               Salt
               Freshly ground black pepper


*Sauce:*    1½  cups Mushroom and Tomato Sauce (page
               60)
             2  tablespoons butter
             1  cup freshly grated Parmesan cheese

Follow the directions for Spinach Pasta on page 110. Roll out the
dough into 2 very thin sheets. In a bowl combine the ricotta
cheese, egg, mozzarella and Parmesan cheeses, nutmeg, and salt
and black pepper to taste, and blend well. Place teaspoons of the
filling over one sheet of the dough at regular intervals about 2
inches apart. Cover with the other sheet of dough and press well
around each mound. With a pastry or ravioli cutter, cut the ravioli
into 2-inch squares. Line them up on a lightly floured board or tray
in a single layer and leave to dry for 15 minutes.

Prepare the mushroom and tomato sauce. Cook the ravioli in
plenty of lightly salted boiling water for 5 to 6 minutes, or until
they are just tender. Transfer to a heated serving bowl. Dot with

butter and spoon the sauce over them. Toss lightly. Serve at once, with grated cheese on the side. *Serves 4.*

*Liguria*

## PANSÔTTI WITH WALNUT SAUCE
### (Pansôtti con salsa di noce)

*Pansôtti* means "potbellied." These "potbellied" ravioli are only found in Liguria, where they are stuffed with *preboggion,* a mixture of wild herbs and greens. *Pansôtti* are always served with walnut sauce.

| | | |
|---|---|---|
| *Filling:* | ¹/₂ | pound beet greens |
| | ¹/₂ | pound Swiss chard |
| | ¹/₂ | pound dandelion leaves |
| | 1 | bunch watercress |
| | 1 | hard-cooked egg yolk |
| | 1 | raw egg, beaten |
| | ¹/₂ | cup ricotta cheese |
| | ¹/₃ | cup freshly grated Parmesan cheese |
| | ¹/₄ | teaspoon freshly grated nutmeg |
| | | Salt |
| | | Freshly ground black pepper |
| | | |
| *Dough:* | 2¹/₂ | cups flour |
| | 3 | eggs |
| | ¹/₂ | teaspoon salt |
| | | |
| *Sauce:* | ¹/₃ | cup shelled walnuts |
| | 2 | tablespoons pine nuts, toasted in a 300°F. oven until golden |

1 garlic clove, crushed
1 small bunch of parsley
⅓ cup ricotta cheese mixed with 3 tablespoons hot water
3 tablespoons olive oil
2 tablespoons butter
½ cup freshly grated Parmesan cheese

Wash the beet greens, Swiss chard, dandelion leaves, and water-cress and cook in a covered saucepan over moderate heat for 5 minutes. The water clinging to the leaves is sufficient to prevent scorching. Drain, squeeze dry, and chop. Mash the egg yolk in a bowl and add the beaten egg, chopped greens, ricotta cheese, ⅓ cup Parmesan cheese, the nutmeg, and salt and black pepper to taste. Blend well together.

Follow the directions for Egg Pasta on page 109. Roll out the dough into 2 very thin sheets. Place teaspoons of the filling over one sheet of the dough at regular intervals about 2 inches apart. Cover with the other sheet of dough and press well around each mound. With a pastry or ravioli cutter, cut the *pansôtti* into 2-inch squares. Line them up on a lightly floured board or tray in a single layer and leave to dry for 15 minutes.

Meanwhile, prepare the sauce.

Mix in a blender the walnuts, pine nuts, garlic, parsley, and ricotta cheese. Gradually add the olive oil to make a smooth sauce with the consistency of sour cream. If the sauce is too thick, add a table-spoon or two of boiling water. Cook the *pansôtti* in plenty of lightly salted boiling water for 5 to 6 minutes, or until they are just tender. Transfer to a heated serving bowl. Dot with the butter and spoon the walnut sauce over them. Toss lightly. Serve at once, with grated cheese on the side. *Serves 4.*

*L o m b a r d y*

## BUCKWHEAT NOODLES WITH VEGETABLES
*(Pizzocheri)*

*Pizzocheri* is a specialty of the Valtellina Valley. The pasta dough is unique as it is made of a combination of buckwheat and wheat flour. It is cooked with a selection of vegetables, usually including potatoes, cabbage, and green beans. The pasta and vegetables are layered with slices of the local Alpine cheese (fontina makes an excellent substitute), sage- and garlic-flavored butter, and grated cheese. The dish is quickly baked in a hot oven until the cheese has melted.

*Dough:*     1¹/₂   **cups buckwheat flour**
       ³/₄   **cup unbleached white flour**
       2   **eggs**
       2   **tablespoons milk**
       ¹/₂   **teaspoon salt**

Combine the buckwheat and unbleached white flour in a bowl. Form a deep well in the center. Drop in 1 egg at a time, then add the milk and the salt. With a fork gradually beat the flour into the egg mixture. Form into a soft ball. Knead for 8 to 10 minutes, until the dough is smooth and elastic. If the dough is too soft, add a little extra flour. Do not add too much flour or the dough will be hard to handle. Wrap the dough in a damp cloth and let it rest for 30 minutes.

Roll out the dough as described on page 110, then cut into strips about 1 inch wide by 3¹/₂ inches long.

½   small head of Savoy cabbage
3   medium-size potatoes, peeled and sliced ¼
    inch thick
¼   pound green beans, cut into 2-inch lengths
    Salt
⅓   cup butter
3   garlic cloves, crushed
1   or 2 fresh sage leaves, chopped
¼   pound fontina cheese, thinly sliced
¾   cup freshly grated Parmesan cheese

Cut the Savoy cabbage into pieces about 2 inches long by 1 inch wide. Bring 4 to 5 quarts of lightly salted water to boil in a large pot. Add the potatoes, Savoy cabbage, and green beans, and cook for 12 to 15 minutes, or until vegetables are almost tender. Add the buckwheat noodles and cook for 4 minutes longer, or until noodles are tender but still firm. Drain and return to the empty pot. Heat the butter in a small pan and sauté the garlic and sage for 2 minutes. Pour butter over the noodles and toss lightly.

Arrange a layer of the noodles and vegetables in a well-buttered shallow baking dish. Cover with slices of fontina cheese and sprinkle with grated Parmesan. Repeat until all the ingredients are used. Finish with fontina cheese and grated Parmesan. Bake in a preheated 400°F. oven for about 10 minutes, or until the noodles are heated through and the cheese has melted. Serve at once, with additional grated cheese on the side, if desired.

The vegetables in this recipe are usually cooked together with the pasta in a large pot of boiling water. If you prefer, you may steam the vegetables separately and combine them with the pasta after it has been cooked. This method prevents the vitamins from being lost in the cooking water. *Serves 6.*

*Campania*

## BAKED LASAGNA WITH EGGPLANT
*(Lasagna al forno)*

*Dough:*  2  cups flour
3  eggs
¹/₂  teaspoon salt

*Filling:*  1  large eggplant, 1 to 1¹/₄ pounds
Salt
¹/₂  cup olive oil
2  cups Tomato Sauce (page 57)
¹/₂  pound mozzarella cheese, thinly sliced
2  cups Béchamel Sauce (page 61)
1  cup freshly grated Parmesan cheese

Peel the eggplant and cut into thin lengthwise slices. Sprinkle with salt. Set in a colander and leave to release the bitter juices for 1 hour. Wash off salt and pat slices dry with paper towels.

Prepare the dough as in the recipe for Egg Pasta on page 109. Let it rest, then roll out fairly thinly. Cut into rectangles about 4¹/₂ inches by 7 inches. Cook about 6 lasagne at a time in plenty of lightly salted boiling water for 3 to 4 minutes. Remove with a slotted spoon and dip into a bowl of cold water. Lay the lasagne flat on a towel. Repeat until all the lasagne are cooked.

Heat the olive oil in a large frying pan and fry the eggplant, a few slices at a time, until golden on both sides. Drain on paper towels. Oil a large shallow baking dish and arrange a layer of lasagne noodles over the bottom. Cover with fried eggplant. Spoon a layer of tomato sauce over the eggplant and cover with slices of mozzarella cheese. Top with a thin layer of béchamel sauce and sprinkle with grated Parmesan cheese. Repeat until all the ingredients are used, finishing with lasagne, béchamel sauce, and grated Parmesan cheese. Bake in a preheated 350°F. oven for 30 to 40 minutes, or until the top is golden. *Serves 4 to 6.*

*Liguria and the North*

# GREEN LASAGNE WITH MUSHROOMS
### *(Lasagne verde pasticciata con funghi)*

*Dough:*   2²/₃  cups flour
            2  eggs
           ¹/₂  pound spinach
           ¹/₂  teaspoon salt

*Filling:*   1¹/₂  cups ricotta cheese
            2  cups Mushroom and Tomato Sauce (page 60)
            2  cups Béchamel Sauce (page 61)
            1  cup freshly grated Parmesan cheese

Prepare the dough as in the recipe for Spinach Pasta on page 110. Let it rest, then roll out fairly thinly. Cut into rectangles about 4¹/₂ inches by 7 inches. Cook about 6 lasagne at a time in plenty of lightly salted boiling water for 3 to 4 minutes. Remove with a slotted spoon and dip into a bowl of cold water. Lay the lasagne flat on a towel. Repeat until all the lasagne are cooked.

Oil a large shallow baking dish and arrange a layer of lasagne over the bottom. Spoon a little ricotta cheese over the bottom. Cover with a little mushroom and tomato sauce, then with béchamel sauce. Sprinkle a little grated Parmesan over the top. Repeat the layers until all the ingredients are used, finishing with lasagne, béchamel sauce, and grated Parmesan cheese. Bake in a preheated 350°F. oven for 30 to 40 minutes, or until the top is golden. *Serves 4 to 6.*

*Piedmont and the North*

# Butterflies with the Whole Garden
### *(Farfalle, tutto giardino)*

*Farfalle* are egg noodles, made into the shape of butterflies.

- 2    tablespoons butter
- 2    tablespoons olive oil
- 2    garlic cloves, crushed
- 1    handful of parsley, chopped
- 1    teaspoon fresh basil, or ¼ teaspoon dried
- 1    teaspoon fresh marjoram, or ¼ teaspoon dried
- 1    leek, thinly sliced
- 1    celery rib, sliced
- 1    small zucchini, sliced
- 1    cup small florets of broccoli
- 1    cup green beans, cut into 1-inch lengths
- 1    cup shelled fresh peas
- 4    ripe plum tomatoes, peeled, seeded, and chopped
- ½    cup Vegetable Broth (page 69)
-      Salt
-      Freshly ground black pepper
- ¾    pound farfalle
- 1    cup freshly grated Parmesan cheese

Heat 1 tablespoon of the butter and the olive oil in a large frying pan and cook the garlic, parsley, basil, and marjoram for 1 minute. Add the leek, celery, zucchini, broccoli, green beans, and peas. Stir well and cook over moderately high heat for 3 minutes. Add the tomatoes and broth. Bring to a boil, cover, and simmer for about

15 minutes, or until the vegetables are just tender and the sauce is thickened. Season with salt and black pepper.

Cook the *farfalle* in plenty of lightly salted boiling water. Drain and transfer to a heated serving bowl. Dot with the remaining butter and pour the vegetable sauce over the *farfalle*. Toss lightly. Serve at once, with grated cheese on the side. *Serves 4 to 6.*

*Liguria*

## EGG NOODLES WITH BEAN SAUCE
### (Fettuccine al stufo)

A specialty of La Spezia

  1   cup dried white beans
  2   tablespoons olive oil
  2   garlic cloves, crushed
  1   small onion, chopped
     Pinch of dried rosemary
  2   tablespoons finely chopped fresh parsley
 ½   cup dry red wine
  2   cups canned plum tomatoes, seeded and chopped
     Salt
     Freshly ground black pepper
1½   pounds egg noodles
  2   tablespoons butter
  1   cup freshly grated Parmesan cheese

Soak the beans in water overnight and drain.

Bring beans to a boil in 2 quarts water, cover, and simmer for 1½ to 2 hours, or until beans are tender. Drain and set aside.

Heat the olive oil in a large frying pan and cook the garlic, onion, rosemary, and parsley over moderate heat for 3 minutes. Add the red wine and cook over high heat until it has evaporated. Add the chopped tomatoes and continue to cook over moderately high heat for 15 minutes, or until the sauce starts to thicken. Add the drained beans, and salt and black pepper to taste. Stir well and simmer for 5 minutes.

Cook the egg noodles in plenty of lightly salted boiling water. Drain and transfer to a heated serving bowl. Dot with the butter and pour the hot sauce over the noodles. Toss lightly. Serve at once, with grated cheese on the side. *Serves 6.*

*Calabria*

## LINGUINE WITH BROCCOLI
### (Linguine con broccoli)

Variations of this dish are found from Calabria to Sicily. The broccoli is simmered in a rich tomato sauce flavored with raisins, pine nuts, and a dash of hot red pepper.

1   large bunch of broccoli
2   tablespoons olive oil
1   garlic clove, crushed
1   small onion, chopped
⅛   teaspoon hot red pepper flakes
½   cup dry red wine

2 cups canned plum tomatoes, seeded and
  chopped
¹/₄ cup pine nuts
¹/₄ cup raisins, soaked in hot water for 10
  minutes
1 cup freshly grated Parmesan cheese
1 pound linguine

Break the broccoli into small flowerets and cut the stems into bite-size pieces. Steam for 7 to 8 minutes, or until broccoli is just tender. Heat the olive oil in a large frying pan and cook the garlic, onion, and hot pepper over moderate heat for 3 minutes. Add the wine and cook over high heat until it has evaporated. Add the tomatoes and cook over moderate heat for 20 to 25 minutes, or until the sauce starts to thicken. Add the pine nuts, raisins, and cooked broccoli and simmer for 5 minutes.

Cook the linguine in plenty of lightly salted boiling water. Drain and transfer to a heated serving bowl. Pour the sauce over linguine and toss lightly. Serve at once, with grated cheese on the side. *Serves 6.*

*Liguria*

## TAGLIATELLE WITH LEEKS
*(Tagliatelle ai porri)*

This is a light and delicious pasta sauce.

1¹/₂ pounds leeks
   3 tablespoons olive oil
   1 handful of parsley, finely chopped
     Pinch of dried rosemary

³/₄   cup canned plum tomatoes, forced through a
        sieve or puréed in a food processor
        Salt
        Freshly ground black pepper
1     pound tagliatelle
2     tablespoons butter
1     cup freshly grated Parmesan cheese

Trim away the roots of the leeks. Cut lengthwise into halves and
carefully wash away the dirt that collects between the leaves. Cut
into slices 1 inch long. Heat the olive oil in a large frying pan and
cook the parsley and rosemary for 1 minute. Add the leeks and
cook gently for 10 minutes. Add the tomato purée, and salt and
black pepper to taste. Cover, and simmer for 30 minutes.

Cook the *tagliatelle* in plenty of lightly salted, boiling water. Drain
and transfer to a heated serving bowl. Dot with the butter and pour
the sauce over the pasta. Toss lightly. Serve at once, with grated
cheese on the side. *Serves 4.*

*Emilia-Romagna*

## EGG NOODLES WITH SWEET
## PEPPERS, PEAS, AND CREAM
### (Fettuccine Ricche alla modenese)

4     tablespoons butter
4     ripe plum tomatoes, peeled, seeded, and
        chopped
1     cup shelled fresh peas
2     sweet red or yellow peppers
        Salt
        Freshly ground black pepper
1     pound egg noodles

$^1/_2$ cup heavy cream, brought to a boil
1 cup freshly grated Parmesan cheese

Heat 2 tablespoons of the butter in a frying pan. Add the tomatoes and peas and cook over moderate heat for 8 minutes. Roast the red peppers under the broiler until the skin is blackened on both sides. Wash under cold water and remove the skins. Cut peppers into small dice and add to the tomato sauce. Simmer for 5 minutes. Season with salt and pepper to taste.

Cook the egg noodles in plenty of lightly salted boiling water. Drain, and transfer to a heating serving bowl. Dot with the remaining butter. Pour the hot cream and the vegetable sauce over the noodles. Toss lightly. Serve at once, with grated cheese on the side. *Serves 4.*

*A p u l i a*

# ORECCHIETTE WITH TURNIP TOPS
### (Orecchiette con cime di rape)

*Orecchiette* are short pasta shaped like "little ears."

$^1/_4$ cup olive oil
2 garlic cloves, crushed
$^1/_8$ teaspoon hot red pepper flakes
2 pounds turnip tops, coarsely chopped
$^3/_4$ pound orecchiette

Heat the olive oil in a large frying pan and cook the garlic and hot pepper for 1 minute. Add the turnip tops, cover, and cook over moderate heat for 7 to 8 minutes, or until they are tender.

Cook the *orecchiette* in plenty of lightly salted boiling water. Drain, and transfer to a heated serving bowl. Cover with the turnip tops, and toss lightly. Serve at once. This dish is served without grated cheese. *Serves 4.*

## Sicily

## MACARONI WITH CAULIFLOWER, RAISINS, AND PINE NUTS
### *(Maccheroni alla cappucina)*

This is an unusual and exotic recipe.

| | |
|---|---|
| 2 | cups small florets of cauliflower |
| 2 | tablespoons olive oil |
| 1 | small onion, chopped |
| 1/2 | teaspoon powdered saffron, dissolved in 1/4 cup boiling water |
| 1/8 | teaspoon ground cuminseed |
| 1/4 | cup pine nuts |
| 1/4 | cup white raisins, soaked in hot water for 10 minutes |
| 3/4 | pound short macaroni |
| 1 | cup freshly grated pecorino cheese |

Steam the cauliflower for 8 to 10 minutes, until just tender. Heat the olive oil in a large frying pan and gently cook the onion for 3 minutes. Add the cauliflower and cook over moderate heat until golden. Add the saffron, cuminseed, pine nuts, and raisins and simmer for 5 minutes.

Cook the macaroni in plenty of lightly salted boiling water. Drain, and transfer to a heated serving bowl. Pour the sauce over the pasta. Toss lightly. Serve at once, with grated cheese on the side. *Serves 4 to 6.*

*Sicily*

## VERMICELLI WITH EGGPLANT AND SWEET PEPPERS
### (Vermicelli alla siracusana)

In this recipe from Syracuse in the south of Sicily, chopped eggplant and roasted sweet peppers are simmered in a tomato sauce that is strongly flavored with olives, capers, and herbs. Caciocavallo cheese is often used in Sicily as a grating cheese instead of pecorino or Parmesan cheese.

1 medium-size eggplant
2 yellow or green sweet peppers
1/4 cup olive oil, approximately
2 garlic cloves, crushed
1/8 teaspoon hot red pepper flakes
1 cup canned plum tomatoes, forced through a sieve or puréed in a food processor
12 Italian or Greek black olives, pitted and chopped
2 tablespoon capers
1 teaspoon fresh basil, or 1/4 teaspoon dried
1 teaspoon fresh oregano, or 1/4 teaspoon dried
Salt
1 pound vermicelli

1  cup freshly grated caciocavallo or pecorino
cheese

Trim the ends of the eggplant but do not peel. Cut into ½-inch
cubes. Roast the sweet peppers under the broiler until they are
blackened all over. Rinse under cold water and remove the skins.
Cut into ½-inch squares. Heat the olive oil in a large frying pan and
cook the garlic and hot pepper for 1 minute. Add the eggplant and
cook, covered, for 5 minutes, until the eggplant is turning golden.
Add the puréed tomatoes and cook over moderate heat for 10
minutes. Add the sweet peppers, olives, capers, basil, oregano, and
salt to taste. Continue to cook for 5 minutes.

Cook the vermicelli in plenty of lightly salted boiling water. Drain,
and transfer to a heated serving bowl. Pour the eggplant sauce over
the pasta. Toss lightly. Serve at once, with grated cheese on the
side. *Serves 4.*

*Sicily*

## BUCATINI WITH EGGPLANT, MUSHROOMS, AND MARSALA
### (Bucatini con melanzana e funghi)

1  eggplant, about ¾ pound
½  cup olive oil
1  small onion, finely chopped
2  tablespoons butter
1  garlic clove, crushed
1  handful of parsley, finely chopped
1  tablespoon fresh basil or ¼ teaspoon dried
½  pound mushrooms, thinly sliced
⅓  cup dry Marsala wine
1  pound bucatini

1 **cup freshly grated Parmesan cheese**

Trim the ends of the eggplant but do not peel. Cut into ¹/₂-inch cubes. Heat the olive oil in a frying pan and cook the onion over moderate heat for 3 minutes. Add the eggplant and cook over moderate heat for 8 to 10 minutes, stirring often, until the eggplant is tender and turning golden. Heat the butter in another frying pan and cook the garlic, parsley, and basil for 1 minute. Add the mushrooms and cook over moderate heat for 5 minutes. Add the Marsala and cook over high heat until the liquid is almost evaporated and the mushrooms are tender. Mix the mushroom sauce with the fried eggplant and simmer together for 5 minutes.

Cook the bucatini in plenty of lightly salted water. Drain, and transfer to a heated serving bowl. Pour the eggplant sauce over the pasta. Serve at once, with grated cheese on the side. *Serves 4.*


*A p u l i a*

## FUSILLI WITH ARUGULA
### *(Fusilli con la ruca)*

———— ❦❦❦ ————

*Fusilli* are short pasta twisted like corkscrews. If arugula is not available, watercress may be used instead.

3 **tablespoons olive oil**
2 **garlic cloves**
1 **small onion**
2 **cups canned plum tomatoes, seeded and chopped**
  **Salt**
  **Freshly ground black pepper**

2   bunches of arugula
1   pound fusilli
1   cup freshly grated pecorino cheese

Heat the olive oil in a large frying pan and cook garlic and onion over moderate heat for 5 minutes, until the onion is translucent. Add the tomatoes and cook over high heat for 15 minutes, or until the sauce is thickened. Season with salt and black pepper to taste. Wash the arugula and trim away the ends. Cook the arugula with the *fusilli* in plenty of lightly salted boiling water. Drain, and transfer to a hot serving bowl. Pour the sauce over the pasta. Toss lightly. Serve at once, with grated cheese on the side. *Serves 4.*

*Sicily*

## MACARONI AND EGGPLANT PIE
### (Pasta 'ncasciata)

Sicilians like baked macaroni and vegetable pies. Although they are not as sophisticated as the lasagne of central Italy, they are particularly delicious and easy to prepare.

1   large eggplant, about 1 pound
    Salt
½   cup olive oil
1   cup shelled fresh peas
2   cups Tomato Sauce (page 57)
¾   pound short macaroni (shells, ziti, penne, etc.)
2   hard-cooked eggs, sliced
6   ounces caciocavallo or mozzarella cheese, sliced

¹/₂  **cup freshly grated pecorino cheese**

Peel the eggplant and cut into slices ¹/₄ inch thick. Sprinkle with salt and set in a colander for 1 hour to release the bitter juices. Wash off the salt and pat slices dry. Fry the eggplant slices quickly in hot oil until golden on both sides. Cook the peas in a little water for 12 to 15 minutes, or until they are tender. Prepare the tomato sauce. Cook the macaroni in plenty of lightly salted boiling water. Drain, and return to the pot. Pour the tomato sauce over the macaroni and toss lightly.

Oil a large shallow baking dish and line the bottom with half of the slices of fried eggplant. Cover with half of the macaroni and tomato sauce. Arrange the slices of hard-cooked eggs on top and scatter the peas over all. Cover with slices of caciocavallo cheese and sprinkle with grated pecorino cheese. Spread remaining fried eggplant over the top and cover with remaining macaroni and sauce. Top with more slices of caciocavallo cheese and sprinkle with remaining pecorino cheese. Bake in a preheated 350°F. oven for 30 to 40 minutes, or until the top is golden and the sauce is bubbling. *Serves 4 to 6.*

# Rice
## *(Il riso)*

Rice was first introduced to Italy by the Saracens. It is mainly grown in the Po Valley in the North, which stretches from Piedmont through Lombardy to the Adriatic Sea.

In Italy, a risotto is always served as a separate course, never as a side dish. Risotto is a very versatile dish, as almost any vegetable can be added to it.

The cooking of risotto is unique. The rice is cooked in butter or oil and herbs for 1 minute, then a ladleful of hot broth is added. The rice is cooked over moderately high heat in an open pot, while the cook watches and stirs, adding more hot broth as the liquid evaporates. The exact cooking time will depend on the age and absorbency of the rice. A little butter is stirred in at the end of cooking and additional grated cheese is served on the side.

Italian arborio rice is the best rice to use for risotto as it produces a creamy texture, while each grain is still *al dente,* or firm to the bite. Precooked or Converted rice is unsuitable for risotto.

*L o m b a r d y*

## S AFFRON  R ICE
### (Risotto alla milanese)

————— ❦ ❦ ❦ —————

Saffron rice, or *risotto alla milanese,* could be called the national dish of Lombardy. Add the saffron towards the end of cooking to retain its delicate flavor. This dish is usually served as a separate course and is sometimes topped with mushrooms or truffles.

> 4   cups Vegetable Broth (page 69), approximately
> 2   tablespoons butter
> 1   small onion, finely chopped
> 1½  cups raw rice
> ½  teaspoon powdered saffron, or ½ teaspoon chopped whole saffron, soaked in ½ cup of the broth
> ¾  cup freshly grated Parmesan cheese
>    Salt
>    Freshly ground black pepper
> 1   truffle, sliced paper-thin (optional)
> 2   tablespoons heavy cream

Bring the broth to a boil in a pan and keep just below the simmer.

Heat the butter in a saucepan and cook the onion over moderate heat for 5 minutes, or until the onion is translucent. Stir in the rice and cook for 1 minute, so each grain is coated with butter. Add a ladleful of the broth. When the liquid is almost evaporated, add another ladleful of broth. Repeat until the rice is tender but still firm. This will take about 25 minutes. About 5 minutes before the end of cooking add the saffron-flavored broth, ¼ cup grated Parmesan cheese, salt and black pepper to taste, and the truffle if used. When the rice is cooked, stir in the heavy cream. Serve at once, with the remaining grated cheese on the side. *Serves 4.*

*L o m b a r d y*

## RICE WITH LEEK AND SWISS CHARD
### *(Ris Porr e erbett)*

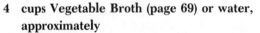

|     |                                                      |
| --- | ---------------------------------------------------- |
| 4   | cups Vegetable Broth (page 69) or water, approximately |
| 1   | leek                                                 |
| 2   | tablespoons olive oil                                |
| 1   | handful of parsley, finely chopped                   |
| 1   | pound Swiss chard, shredded                          |
| 1½  | cups raw rice                                        |
|     | Salt                                                 |
|     | Freshly ground black pepper                          |
| 2   | tablespoons butter                                   |
| 1   | cup freshly grated Parmesan cheese                   |

Bring the broth to a boil in a pan and keep just below the simmer. Cut away the root end of the leek and cut lengthwise into halves. Wash away all the dirt that collects between the leaves and cut leek into thin slices. Use the whole of the leek, including the dark green tops. Heat the olive oil in a saucepan and add the parsley, leek, and Swiss chard. Cook, covered, over moderate heat for 10 minutes, stirring occasionally so the vegetables cook evenly. Stir in the rice and add a ladleful of broth. Cook until the liquid is almost evaporated. Add another ladleful of broth and repeat until the rice is tender but still firm. The finished risotto should be slightly creamy and the liquid evaporated. Season with salt and black pepper to taste. Stir in the butter. Serve at once, with grated cheese on the side. *Serves 4.*

*Tuscany*

## RICE WITH SUMMER VEGETABLES
### *(Risotto d'estate)*

|  |  |
|---|---|
| 4 | cups Vegetable Broth (page 69), approximately |
| 1/4 | pound asparagus |
| 3 | tablespoons olive oil |
| 1 | small onion, chopped |
| 1 | tablespoon fresh basil, or 1/2 teaspoon dried |
| 1 | zucchini, sliced |
| 1 | cup shelled fresh peas |
| 6 | plum tomatoes, peeled, seeded, and chopped |
|  | Salt |
|  | Freshly ground black pepper |
| 1 1/2 | cups raw rice |
| 1/2 | teaspoon powdered saffron, or 1/2 teaspoon whole saffron, soaked in 1/2 cup of the broth |
| 2 | tablespoons butter |
| 1 | cup freshly grated Parmesan cheese |

Bring the broth to a boil in a pan and keep just below the simmer.

Trim the ends of the asparagus and peel the stalks with a sharp knife or vegetable peeler up to about 2 inches from the tips. Cut diagonally into 1-inch lengths. Heat the olive oil in a saucepan and cook the onion and basil over moderate heat for 2 minutes. Add the zucchini, asparagus, peas, and ¼ cup of broth. Cover, and simmer for 10 minutes. Add the chopped tomatoes and salt and black pepper to taste and simmer for 10 minutes more. Add the rice and a ladleful of broth and cook until the liquid is almost evaporated. Add another ladleful of broth and repeat until the rice is tender but still firm. About 5 minutes before the end of cooking add the saffron-flavored broth and stir well. The finished risotto should be slightly creamy and the liquid evaporated. Stir in the butter. Serve at once, with the grated cheese on the side. *Serves 4 to 6.*

*Veneto*

# RICE WITH RAISINS AND PINE NUTS
*(Riso co la ua)*

This is simple, exotic, and delicious.

    5   cups Vegetable Broth (page 69),
        approximately
    2   tablespoons olive oil
    1   garlic clove, crushed
    1   small onion, finely chopped
    1   handful of parsley, chopped
    ½   cup dry white wine
    2   cups raw rice
    ½   cup raisins
    ¼   cup pine nuts
        Salt
        Freshly ground black pepper

2   tablespoons butter
³/₄   cup freshly grated Parmesan cheese

Bring the broth to a boil in a pan and keep just below the simmer. Heat the olive oil in a saucepan and cook the garlic, onion, and parsley over moderate heat for 5 minutes, or until the onion is translucent. Add the white wine and cook over high heat until it has evaporated. Stir in the rice. Add a ladleful of broth and cook until the liquid is almost evaporated. Add another ladleful of broth, the raisins, and pine nuts and repeat until the rice is tender but still firm. Season with salt and black pepper to taste. Stir in the butter. Serve at once, with grated cheese on the side. *Serves 4 to 6.*

*L a z i o*

### R I C E   W I T H   L E N T I L S
*(Risotto con lenticchie)*

Use small green lentils for this dish.

1¹/₂   cups green lentils
3   tablespoons olive oil
2   garlic cloves, crushed
1   small onion, chopped
1   celery rib, thinly sliced
2   tablespoons finely chopped parsley
1   cup canned plum tomatoes, seeded and
    chopped
    Salt
    Freshly ground black pepper
1¹/₂   cups raw rice
2   tablespoons butter
³/₄   cup freshly grated pecorino romano cheese

Soak the lentils in water overnight and drain. Bring the lentils to a boil in about 5 cups water and simmer, covered, for 1½ hours, or until they are tender.

Heat the olive oil in another saucepan and gently cook the garlic, onion, celery, and parsley for 5 minutes. Add the chopped tomatoes and cook over high heat for 10 minutes, until the sauce is starting to thicken. Add the lentils and their cooking water (which should be about 3½ cups), and salt and black pepper to taste. Pour in the rice and simmer, covered, for 8 to 10 minutes, or until the rice is tender but still firm and most of the liquid is evaporated. This risotto should not be too dry. Stir in the butter. Serve at once, with grated cheese on the side. *Serves 6.*

*Veneto*

## RICE AND PEAS
### *(Risi e bisi)*

This is the most famous dish of the Veneto region. To retain the special quality of this dish, fresh peas are a must. Choose the tiniest, sweetest peas that you can find.

    4   cups Vegetable Broth (page 69) or water,
        approximately
    2   tablespoons olive oil
    1   small onion, finely chopped
    1   celery rib, thinly sliced
    2   tablespoons chopped fresh parsley
 1½   cups raw rice
    2   cups shelled young tender peas
        Salt

Freshly ground black pepper
2  tablespoons butter
³/₄  cup freshly grated Parmesan cheese

Bring the broth to a boil in a pan and keep just below a simmer. Heat the olive oil in a saucepan and cook the onion, celery, and parsley over moderate heat until they are turning golden. Stir in the rice and cook for 1 minute, so each grain is coated with oil. Add a ladleful of broth and cook until the liquid is almost evaporated. Add another ladleful of broth, the peas, and salt and black pepper to taste. Continue adding broth until the rice is tender but still firm and the liquid is evaporated. Stir in the butter. Serve at once, with grated cheese on the side. *Serves 4.*

*Veneto*

## Rice with Fennel
*(Risi coi fenoci)*

The Venetians like their risottos especially creamy. In Italian they say wavy or *ondosa.* Rice with fennel is particularly delicate and very delicious. Try it with a chilled glass of dry white wine, such as a Soave.

4  cups Vegetable Broth (page 69),
     approximately
1  large fennel bulb, about ³/₄ pound
2  tablespoons olive oil
1  small onion, chopped
1¹/₂  cups raw rice
     Salt
     Freshly ground black pepper

2 tablespoons butter
³/₄ cup freshly grated Parmesan cheese

Bring the broth to a boil in a pan and keep just below a simmer. Trim away the stems and tough outer leaves of the fennel and cut the bulb into small dice. Heat the olive oil in a saucepan and cook the onion and fennel over moderate heat until they are starting to turn golden. Add the rice and cook for 1 minute, so each grain is coated with oil. Add a ladleful of broth, and salt and black pepper to taste, and cook until the liquid is almost evaporated. Add another ladleful of broth and repeat until the rice is tender but firm. Stir in the butter and serve at once, with grated cheese on the side. *Serves 4.*

*Liguria*

## Rice with Zucchini and Pesto
### (Risotto con zucchini e pesto)

4 cups Vegetable Broth (page 69) or water, approximately
3 small zucchini, about ³/₄ pound altogether
2 garlic cloves, crushed
2 tablespoons finely chopped parsley
1¹/₂ cups raw rice
2 tablespoons butter
3 tablespoons Pesto Sauce (page 62)
¹/₂ cup freshly grated Parmesan cheese

Bring the broth to a boil and keep just below a simmer. Trim the ends of the zucchini and cut vegetables into thin slices. Heat the olive oil in a saucepan and cook garlic and parsley for 1 minute. Add the zucchini and cook over moderately high heat until golden on both sides. Add the rice and cook for 1 minute so each grain is coated with oil. Add a ladleful of broth. Repeat until the rice is tender but still firm and all the liquid is evaporated. Stir in the butter and pesto sauce. Serve at once with grated cheese on the side. *Serves 4.*

*L o m b a r d y*

# ITALIAN FRIED RICE
### (Risotto al salto)

This is more like a rice pancake than fried rice. Leftover rice is combined with an egg yolk and diced mozzarella cheese, and fried on both sides until crisp and golden.

2   cups leftover Saffron Rice (page 134)
1   egg yolk
⅓   cup small dice of mozzarella cheese
2   tablespoons olive oil
⅓   cup freshly grated Parmesan cheese

Combine the leftover rice, egg yolk, and mozzarella cheese in a bowl. Mix lightly without mashing the rice. Heat 2 tablespoons olive oil in a frying pan and add the rice mixture. It should be about ½-inch thick. Cook over moderate heat for 5 to 6 minutes or until the bottom is golden. Place a saucepan lid or plate over the frying pan and quickly turn the pan over. Slide the rice back into the frying pan and cook until the rice is golden on the other side. Cut into wedges. Serve with grated cheese on the side. *Serves 2 to 3.*

*Lombardy*

## RICE WITH ONIONS
*(La Risotta)*

This dish should be very liquid and creamy and is therefore known by the feminine nickname of *la risotta*.

2¹/₂  cups Vegetable Broth (page 69)
3  tablespoons butter
2  pounds onions, finely chopped
³/₄  cup raw rice
¹/₂  teaspoon powdered saffron or chopped whole saffron, soaked in ¹/₂ cup of the broth
Salt
Fresh ground black pepper
2  tablespoons heavy cream
³/₄  cup freshly grated Parmesan cheese

Bring the broth to a boil in a pan and keep just below a simmer. Heat the butter in a saucepan and cook the onions over moderate heat for 15 minutes, or until they start to turn light brown. Stir in the rice and cook for 1 minute so each grain is coated with butter. Add a ladleful of broth. When the liquid is almost evaporated, add another ladleful of broth. Repeat until the rice is tender but still firm. This will take about 25 minutes.

About 5 minutes before the end of cooking add the saffron-flavored broth and salt and black pepper to taste. Do not let the rice dry out. Add a little more hot broth, if necessary. When the rice is cooked, stir in 2 tablespoons heavy cream. Serve at once, with grated cheese on the side. *Serves 3 to 4.*

*Piedmont*

## SPINACH AND RICE PIE
### *(Turta)*

| | |
|---|---|
| 1 | pound fresh spinach |
| 4 | cups Vegetable Broth (page 69), approximately |
| 2 | tablespoons olive oil |
| 1 | small onion, finely chopped |
| 1 | handful of parsley, finely chopped |
| 1 | teaspoon fresh marjoram, or ¼ teaspoon dried |
| 1½ | cups raw rice |
| 4 | tablespoons butter |
| 5 | eggs, beaten |
| 1 | cup freshly grated Parmesan cheese |
| ¼ | teaspoon freshly grated nutmeg |
| | Salt |
| | Freshly ground black pepper |

Wash the spinach and cook in a covered saucepan over moderate heat for 5 minutes. The water clinging to the leaves is sufficient to prevent scorching. Drain, squeeze dry, and chop. Set aside. Bring the broth to a boil in a pan and keep just below a simmer. Heat the olive oil in a saucepan and gently cook the onion, parsley, and marjoram for 5 minutes, or until the onion is translucent. Stir in the rice and cook for 1 minute so each grain is coated with oil. Add a ladleful of broth and cook until the liquid is almost evaporated. Add another ladleful of broth and repeat until the rice is tender but still firm and all the liquid is evaporated. Stir in 2 tablespoons of butter. Transfer the rice to a mixing bowl and let it cool slightly. Add the beaten eggs, the chopped spinach, ½ cup Parmesan cheese, the nutmeg, and salt and black pepper to taste. Mix well together. Pour into a well-buttered deep baking dish or soufflé dish and smooth the top with the back of a spoon. Melt remaining 2 tablespoons butter and dribble over the top. Bake in a preheated

375°F. oven for 30 to 40 minutes, or until the top is crisp and golden. Serve with remaining grated cheese on the side. *Serves 6.*


## *Polenta*
### *(Polenta)*

Polenta is a simple cornmeal mush that is one of the staple foods of Piedmont, Lombardy, and the regions of the Veneto.

Polenta comes from the Roman "puls" or "pulmentum," a kind of porridge or crumbly cake that was made originally by the Etruscans.

Polenta is usually made from cornmeal, but there is a version from the Valtellina Valley in Lombardy called *polenta taragna* that is made with buckwheat flour.

Polenta is traditionally made in a paiolo or unlined copper kettle. It is always stirred with a wooden spoon or stick. Italian cornmeal, or *farina gialla,* comes in various degrees of fineness. I prefer the coarse variety found in Italian groceries, but American cornmeal may be used instead.


*The North*

### POLENTA
### *(Polenta)*

———— ❦ ❦ ❦ ————

  7   cups water, or more as needed
1¹/₄  teaspoons salt
  2   cups coarse cornmeal

Bring the water to a boil in a large, heavy pot. Add salt and reduce the heat to a simmer. Slowly pour in the cornmeal in a very thin stream, stirring constantly to prevent lumps from forming. Continue stirring for at least 45 minutes. If the polenta becomes too thick, add a little more boiling water. The polenta is cooked when it comes away from the sides of the pan and has lost any slight bitter taste.

The polenta may be eaten immediately with butter and cheese, or the sauce of your choice, or it may be spread out on a work surface and left to harden. When cool, the polenta may be sliced like a cake, and used as the foundation for various delicious pies or fritters.

*Veneto*

## POLENTA AND CHEESE PIE
*(Polenta pastizzada)*

1   recipe Polenta (preceding recipe)
½   pound fontina or Gruyère cheese, thinly sliced
2   cups Tomato Sauce (page 57)
1   cup freshly grated Parmesan cheese

Prepare the polenta and spread on a wooden board or baking sheet in a thin layer about ½ inch thick. Leave to cool. When cold cut into slices.

Butter a baking dish and arrange layers of polenta slices over the bottom. Cover with a layer of fontina cheese. Top with tomato sauce and sprinkle with grated cheese. Repeat the layers until all the ingredients are used, finishing with tomato sauce and grated cheese. Bake in a preheated 375°F. oven for 20 minutes, or until the top is golden and the sauce is bubbling. *Serves 6.*

*Piedmont*

## POLENTA PIE WITH MUSHROOMS
*(Polenta pasticciata con funghi)*

    1   recipe Polenta (page 145)
    1   tablespoon butter
    1   tablespoon olive oil
    1   pound mushrooms, thinly sliced
    2   cups Béchamel Sauce (page 61)
   1/2  cup grated Gruyère cheese
    1   cup freshly grated Parmesan cheese

Prepare the polenta and spread on a wooden board or baking tin in a thin layer 1/2 inch thick. Leave to cool. When cold, cut into slices.

Heat the butter and olive oil in a frying pan and cook the mushrooms over moderate heat for 5 minutes, or until they are tender. Meanwhile, prepare the béchamel sauce. Remove from the heat and stir in the Gruyère cheese. Butter a baking dish and arrange a layer of polenta slices over the bottom. Cover with a layer of mushrooms. Spoon the cheese sauce over and sprinkle with grated cheese. Repeat the layers until all the ingredients are used, finishing with the cheese sauce and grated cheese. Bake in a preheated 375°F. oven until the top is golden and the sauce is bubbling. *Serves 6.*

*Emilia-Romagna*

# POLENTA AND BEANS
### *(Calzagatti)*

This is a specialty of Modena.

1   **cup dried white beans**
     **Salt**
2   **tablespoons olive oil**
2   **garlic cloves, crushed**
1   **small onion, finely chopped**
1   **cup canned plum tomatoes, seeded and chopped**
2   **cups coarse cornmeal**
4   **tablespoons butter**

Soak the beans in water overnight and drain.

Bring beans to a boil in unsalted boiling water and cook, covered, for 1½ hours, or until they are tender. Season with salt. Pour off and reserve the cooking liquid. Heat the olive oil in a frying pan and cook the garlic and onion over moderate heat for 5 minutes, or until the onion is translucent. Add the tomatoes and cook over high heat for 10 minutes, until the sauce starts to thicken. Add to the drained beans and set aside.

Add sufficient water to the reserved bean cooking liquid to make 7 cups water. Bring to a boil in a heavy pot. Add 1¼ teaspoons salt and reduce the heat to a simmer. Slowly pour in the cornmeal in a very thin stream, stirring constantly to prevent lumps from forming. Continue stirring for at least 45 minutes. If the polenta becomes too thick add a little more boiling water. Just before the end of cooking remove polenta from the heat and stir in the beans with tomato sauce and the butter. Return to the heat and cook for 5 minutes longer, stirring constantly. Serve at once.

*Calzagatti* may also be cooled, cut into squares, and deep-fried in hot oil until golden and crispy. *Serves 6.*


*Piedmont*

## FRIED POLENTA SANDWICHES
### *(Polenta in carozza)*

———— 🌾🌾🌾 ————

  1  recipe Polenta (page 145)
 ¹/₂ pound fontina cheese
    Flour
  2  eggs, beaten
    Bread crumbs
    Oil for frying

Prepare the polenta and spread on a wooden board or baking sheet in a thin layer about ¹/₂ inch thick. Cut into 3-inch rounds with a glass or cookie cutter. Cut the fontina cheese to rounds of the same size as the polenta and sandwich each cheese slice between rounds of polenta. Press well together so the filling will not fall out. Dip the sandwiches into flour, then into beaten eggs, then into bread crumbs. Fry in hot oil until golden on both sides. Drain on paper towels and serve at once. *Serves 4 to 6.*


## Dumplings
### *(Gnocchi)*

Most regions of Italy have their own versions of gnocchi. They are usually made with mashed potatoes or semolina flour, or a mixture of spinach and Ricotta cheese. In Liguria gnocchi are sometimes made with chestnut flour and served with walnut sauce. *Gnocchi di zucca*, a specialty of Lombardy, are made with mashed pumpkin, egg, flour, cinnamon, and crushed macaroons.

Gnocchi, like pasta, are cooked in plenty of lightly salted, boiling water. Just before they are cooked they float to the surface where they can be easily removed with a slotted spoon and the next batch put on to cook.

Gnocchi may be served simply with butter and cheese, or with the sauce of your choice.

*C a m p a n i a*

## POTATO DUMPLINGS
### *(Strangugli or Strangulaprievete)*

———— ❧❧❧ ————

There are many versions of potato dumplings in Italy. These are made without eggs. The exact amount of flour needed will depend upon the moisture content of the potatoes. Too much flour will make the dumplings tough and heavy. To test, try one dumpling in boiling water to be sure that it holds its shape without falling apart.

2  pounds "old" potatoes
1³/₄  cups unbleached white flour, approximately
1  teaspoon salt
2  cups Tomato Sauce (page 57), hot
1  cup freshly grated pecorino cheese

Boil the potatoes in lightly salted water for 20 minutes, or until they are tender. Drain. When they are cool enough to handle, remove the skins. Force through a sieve or potato ricer and let fall on a lightly floured board or work surface. While the potatoes are still warm, work in the flour and salt to make a stiff dough. Roll dough into long cylinders about the thickness of your finger, then cut into 1-inch lengths. Press each piece with your index finger against the inside of a fork, forming a crescent shape with an indent on the inside where your finger was and ridges on the outside from the fork.

Drop about half of the gnocchi into a large pot of lightly salted boiling water. The gnocchi will float to the surface when they are cooked, in less than 1 minute. Remove with a slotted spoon and transfer to a heated serving bowl. Spoon a little hot tomato sauce over them. Repeat with remaining gnocchi and cover with remaining sauce. Serve at once, with grated cheese on the side. *Serves 6.*

*L a z i o*

## BAKED SEMOLINA GNOCCHI
### *(Gnocchi alla romana)*

  2 cups milk
  2 cups water
  1 cup semolina flour
 ¹/₄ pound butter, softened
 ¹/₈ teaspoon freshly grated nutmeg
 ¹/₂ teaspoon salt
  2 egg yolks
 1¹/₄ cups freshly grated Parmesan cheese

Bring the milk and water to a boil in a saucepan over moderate heat. Slowly pour in the semolina flour in a thin stream, stirring constantly. Add 2 tablespoons of the butter, the nutmeg, and ¹/₂ teaspoon salt, and cook for 15 minutes longer, stirring frequently.

Remove from the heat. Add the egg yolks and ¼ cup of the grated cheese. Blend well together. Moisten a baking sheet with cold water and pour in the semolina mixture. Spread it out evenly with a wet spatula into a layer about ¼ inch thick. Cool for 1 hour, or until the semolina is quite firm.

Cut cold semolina into 1½-inch rounds, with a cookie cutter or a small drinking glass. Arrange 2 or 3 layers of gnocchi rounds in a well-buttered baking dish and sprinkle each layer with Parmesan cheese and dots of butter. Bake in a preheated 375°F. oven for 15 to 20 minutes or until the gnocchi are golden. *Serves 6.*

*Tuscany*

## Swiss Chard and Ricotta Dumplings
### (Strozzapreti alla fiorentina)

*Strozzapreti,* like the Neapolitan *Strangula-prievete,* means "priest strangler." The name probably alludes to the clergy's reputed gluttony and how priests were said to eat these dumplings so quickly that they would choke on them. Most recipes for *Strozzapreti* add a little flour into the dumpling mixture, but I find that if you squeeze most of the moisture out of the cooked Swiss chard, no flour is necessary. Simply dipping the gnocchi into flour before cooking is sufficient to hold them together. The cooking time is very quick, about 3 minutes.

**2   pounds Swiss chard**

1½ cups ricotta cheese
2 egg yolks
⅔ cup Parmesan cheese
¼ teaspoon freshly grated nutmeg
⅛ teaspoon ground cinnamon
Salt
Freshly ground black pepper
Flour
6 tablespoons butter

Cook the Swiss chard in a covered saucepan over moderate heat for 5 minutes. The water clinging to the leaves is sufficient to prevent scorching. Drain, squeeze dry, and chop coarsely. Place chard in a mixing bowl with the ricotta cheese, egg yolks, ⅓ cup Parmesan cheese, the nutmeg, cinnamon, and salt and black pepper to taste. Blend well together. Cover the bowl and refrigerate for 2 hours.

Form the mixture into long sausage shapes about ¾ inch in diameter, and cut into 1-inch lengths. Dip the gnocchi lightly into flour and drop about half of the dumplings into rapidly boiling, lightly salted water. The dumplings will float to the surface when they are cooked. Remove with a slotted spoon and transfer to a hot serving bowl. Dot with half the butter and sprinkle with half of the remaining grated cheese. Repeat with the remaining dumplings and top with the remaining butter and grated cheese. *Serves 4.*

# MAIN COURSES

## Pies and Tarts
### (Torte e crostate)

Pies and tarts make excellent lunch or supper dishes, served with a salad and followed by dessert. They are usually made of unsweetened short-crust pastry or a paper-thin strudel-type pastry.

Pies may be filled with vegetables in cream sauces, cheese and vegetable custards, and some stews or gratins. The pies and tarts in this chapter are made with short-crust pastry or thawed filo pastry, which makes an excellent substitute for strudel pastry. If you are using frozen filo pastry, thaw it for a minimum of 2 hours before using so the sheets can be easily separated. If 2 sheets stick together, use them as if they were one. Simply brush them with oil and continue. Work as quickly as possible as filo pastry dries out very quickly.

## SHORT-CRUST PASTRY
### (Pasta Frolla)

A good short-crust pastry is crisp and buttery when baked. Work very quickly while you make this pastry. If the dough is worked too much it becomes hard to handle. Whole-

wheat pastry flour or unbleached white flour
or a combination of both may be used.

1¼  cups whole-wheat pastry or unbleached
     white flour
 ¼   teaspoon salt
 ¼   pound chilled butter, cut into very small
     cubes
 3   or 4 tablespoons ice water, approximately

Combine the flour, salt, and butter in a mixing bowl. Rub the butter into the flour with your fingertips, until the mixture resembles coarse bread crumbs. Working very quickly, sprinkle in enough ice water to form a soft ball of dough. The dough should not be sticky. Wrap in wax paper and refrigerate for 30 minutes before rolling. *Makes enough for a 9- or 10-inch pie shell.*

**Rolling out
the dough**

Place the dough on a lightly floured board and knead it briefly. Roll out into a circle about 12 inches in diameter and ⅛ inch thick. (Any extra dough can be used for tartlets.) Carefully roll the dough around the rolling pin and unroll it onto a well-buttered pie plate. Trim away any excess dough and flute the edges with a fork. Prick the bottom in a few places. Cover the dough with a sheet of aluminum foil and fill with dried beans or aluminum pie pellets. This keeps the pie shell from puffing up while baking.

**For a partially baked
pie shell**

Preheat oven to 400°F. and bake the pastry for 8 to 10 minutes. The pastry should have shrunk away from the sides of the pie plate. Remove from the oven and carefully remove the foil and beans or pellets.

*For a fully
baked pie
shell*

Return to the oven. Prick the bottom again and bake for another 8 to 10 minutes, until the pastry is a very light brown.

*L i g u r i a*

## EASTER PIE
### *(La torta pasqualina)*

———— ❦❦❦ ————

*La torta pasqualina* is a famous Genovese specialty. It is made of layers of paper-thin noodle pastry filled with Swiss chard and a ricotta-type cheese called *quagliata*. Depressions are made in the cheese at regular intervals and an egg is broken into each. More layers of pastry are spread on top and the whole is baked in the oven. Frozen filo pastry, available in many gourmet stores and supermarkets, makes this elaborate pie easy to prepare. The accomplished cook who wants to prepare the pastry at home should note that it is not possible to make the pastry sheets as thin as commercial filo pastry, so less sheets are required.

*Pastry:*

| | |
|---|---|
| 1 | pound unbleached white flour |
| 1/2 | teaspoon salt |
| 3/4 | cup water, approximately |
| 1 | tablespoon olive oil |

Place the flour and salt in a mixing bowl. Make a well in the center and add the water and olive oil. Work into a soft dough. Knead well for about 15 minutes, until the dough is smooth and elastic, adding a little more water if necessary. The exact quantity of water depends upon the absorbency of the flour. Wrap the dough in a damp cloth and let it rest for 1 hour.

*Filling:*   2   pounds Swiss chard or spinach
$\frac{1}{2}$   cup olive oil, approximately
1   teaspoon fresh marjoram, or $\frac{1}{2}$ teaspoon dried
$\frac{3}{4}$   cup freshly grated Parmesan cheese
$1\frac{1}{2}$   cups ricotta cheese
$\frac{1}{4}$   cup heavy cream
1   tablespoon unbleached white flour
$\frac{1}{4}$   teaspoon ground cinnamon
$\frac{1}{4}$   teaspoon freshly grated nutmeg
Salt
Freshly ground black pepper
6   eggs
2   tablespoons melted butter

Wash the Swiss chard and cook in a covered saucepan over moderate heat for 5 minutes. Drain, squeeze dry, and chop coarsely. Heat 2 tablespoons of the olive oil in a saucepan, add the marjoram and Swiss chard, and cook gently for 5 minutes. Remove from the heat and stir in $\frac{1}{4}$ cup Parmesan cheese. Set aside. In a bowl combine the ricotta cheese, cream, flour, cinnamon, nutmeg, and salt and black pepper to taste and blend well.

Divide the dough into 10 equal portions and roll each portion out on a lightly floured board to a sheet as thin as possible. Stretch the dough out with the hands into a rectangle about 13 × 9 inches. Place a sheet of pastry (or filo pastry if used) over the bottom of a well-oiled baking pan about 11 × 7 inches, at least 2 inches deep. Brush the top with olive oil and place another sheet of pastry on top. Repeat until 6 sheets of pastry are used (10 sheets if using filo pastry). Spread the Swiss chard evenly over the pastry and cover with the ricotta cheese mixture. With the back of a spoon, make indentations over the filling deep enough to hold an egg. Break 1 egg into each hollow. Sprinkle the top lightly with salt, black pepper, and remaining grated cheese. Dribble the melted butter over the top. Very carefully place a sheet of pastry or filo pastry over the top. Do not press down. Brush lightly with olive oil. Repeat with remaining sheets of pastry. Use as light a hand as possible. Bake in a preheated 325°F. oven for 1 hour, or until the top is golden. *Serves 6.*

*L i g u r i a*

## SWISS CHARD PIE
### *(Torta d'erbette)*

———— ❦❦❦ ————

A simpler version of *La torta pasqualina.*

| Pastry | 2 | pounds Swiss chard, spinach, or beet greens |
|---|---|---|
| | 2 | tablespoons butter |
| | 1 | handful of parsley, chopped |
| | 1 | leek, thinly sliced |
| | 2 | cups ricotta cheese |
| | 3 | eggs |
| | 1/4 | cup freshly grated Parmesan cheese |
| | 1/8 | teaspoon freshly grated nutmeg |
| | | Salt |
| | | Freshly ground black pepper |
| | | Olive oil |

Follow the recipe for the pastry for Easter pie (previous recipe), or use 15 sheets of thawed filo pastry. Wash the Swiss chard carefully and cook in a covered saucepan over moderate heat for 5 minutes. Drain, squeeze dry, and coarsely chop. Heat the butter in a large frying pan and cook the parsley and leek over moderate heat for 8 to 10 minutes, or until the leek is tender. Add the chopped Swiss chard and cook for 1 minute. Mix the ricotta cheese, eggs, and Parmesan cheese in a large bowl. Add the nutmeg and salt and black pepper to taste, and blend well.

Place a sheet of the pastry or filo pastry over the bottom of a well-oiled baking pan about 2 inches deep. Brush the top with olive oil and place another sheet of pastry on top. Repeat until 6 sheets of pastry (or 10 sheets of filo pastry) are used. Combine the cooked Swiss chard mixture with the ricotta cheese and spread over the pastry. Place a sheet of pastry or filo pastry on top and brush lightly with olive oil. Repeat with the remaining sheets of pastry. Bake in a preheated 350°F. oven for 30 to 40 minutes, or until the top is golden and the pie is puffed. *Serves 6 to 8.*

*Liguria*

## Mushroom and Zucchini Pie
### *(La torta di funghi e zucchini)*

Another delicious vegetable pie from Liguria.

| Pastry | | |
|---|---|---|
| | 2 | tablespoons butter |
| | 2 | tablespoons finely chopped fresh parsley |
| | 1 | pound mushrooms, thinly sliced |
| | ³/₄ | cup olive oil, approximately |
| | 4 | small zucchini, 1 to 1¹/₄ pounds altogether, thinly sliced |
| | 2 | cups ricotta cheese |
| | 3 | eggs |
| | ¹/₂ | cup freshly grated Parmesan cheese |
| | ¹/₈ | teaspoon freshly grated nutmeg |

**Salt**
**Freshly ground black pepper**

Follow the recipe for the pastry for Easter Pie (page 156), or use 15 sheets of thawed filo pastry. Heat the butter in a large frying pan and cook the parsley for 1 minute. Add the mushrooms and cook over moderate heat for 5 minutes, or until just tender. Set aside. Heat 3 tablespoons of the olive oil in another large frying pan and cook the zucchini over moderately high heat until golden on both sides. Set aside. Mix the ricotta cheese, eggs, and Parmesan cheese in a large bowl. Add the nutmeg, and salt and black pepper to taste.

Place a sheet of pastry or filo pastry over the bottom of a well-oiled baking pan about 2 inches deep. Brush the top with olive oil and place another sheet of pastry on top. Repeat until 6 sheets of pastry (or 10 sheets of filo pastry) are used. Cover with the slices of fried zucchini. Spread the ricotta cheese mixture over the zucchini. Top with the fried mushrooms. Place a sheet of pastry or filo pastry over the top and brush lightly with olive oil. Repeat with remaining sheets of pastry. Bake in a preheated 350°F. oven for 30 to 40 minutes, or until the top is golden and the pie is puffed. *Serves 6 to 8.*

*Valle d'Aosta*

### ONION TART
*(Crostate di cipolle)*

This is one of my favorite tarts. The onions should be cooked very slowly, without browning, until they are reduced to almost a purée, then add the eggs and cream.

2   pounds onions
2   tablespoons olive oil
1   tablespoon butter
2   eggs
1   cup heavy cream
¼   cup freshly grated Parmesan cheese
⅛   teaspoon freshly grated nutmeg
    Salt
    Freshly ground black pepper
    9-inch partially baked pie shell

Peel the onions and slice very thin. Heat the olive oil and butter in
a large frying pan and add the onions. Cover and cook gently for
25 to 30 minutes, or until they are very soft. Do not brown. Beat
the eggs and cream together in a bowl. Add the Parmesan cheese,
nutmeg, salt and black pepper to taste, and the onions. Pour into
the partially baked pie shell. Bake in a preheated 375°F. oven for
30 minutes, or until the tart is lightly browned and puffed. *Serves
4 to 6.*

*Emilia-Romagna*

## MUSHROOM TART
### *(Crostata di funghi)*

3   tablespoons butter
1   small onion, chopped
2   tablespoons finely chopped parsley
1   tablespoon fresh marjoram, or ¼ teaspoon
    dried
1   pound fresh mushrooms, thinly sliced
3   tablespoons dry Marsala wine
3   eggs

1½   cups heavy cream
Salt
Freshly ground black pepper
9-inch partially baked pie shell

Heat the butter in a large frying pan and cook the onion, parsley, and marjoram for 1 minute. Add the mushrooms and cook for 5 minutes. Add the Marsala, raise the heat, and cook until wine has evaporated. Add salt and black pepper to taste. Beat the eggs and cream together in a bowl and stir in the mushroom mixture. Pour into the partially baked pie shell. Bake in the center of a preheated 375°F. oven for 30 minutes, or until the tart is lightly browned and puffed. *Serves 4 to 6.*

*Lombardy and the North*

## PEA AND LETTUCE TART
*(Crostata di piselli e lattuga)*

1   pound peas, shelled
1   tablespoon olive oil
2   tablespoons butter
1   head of Boston lettuce, shredded
1   handful of fresh parsley, chopped
3   eggs
1   cup heavy cream
½   cup milk
⅓   cup freshly grated Parmesan cheese
Salt
Freshly ground black pepper
9-inch partially baked pie shell

Cook the peas in lightly salted boiling water for 10 to 30 minutes, until they are tender. The exact cooking time depends on their age and size. Heat the olive oil and butter in a large frying pan. Add the lettuce and parsley and cook, covered, over moderate heat for 5 minutes, or until the lettuce is wilted. Raise the heat, if necessary, to evaporate any excess moisture. Add the cooked peas, stir well, and cook for 1 minute.

Beat the eggs, cream, and milk together in a bowl. Add the Parmesan cheese, salt and black pepper to taste, and the pea mixture and blend well. Pour into the partially baked pie shell. Bake in the center of a preheated 375°F. oven for 30 minutes, or until the tart is lightly browned and puffed. *Serves 4 to 6.*

*E m i l i a - R o m a g n a*

## ASPARAGUS TART
### *(Crostata di asparagii)*

1 pound asparagus
3 eggs
1 cup heavy cream
1/2 cup milk
1/2 cup freshly grated Parmesan cheese
1/8 teaspoon freshly grated nutmeg
Salt
Freshly ground black pepper
9-inch partially baked pie shell

Trim the tough ends of the asparagus and peel the stalks with a sharp knife or vegetable peeler up to about 2 inches from the tips. Steam for 20 minutes, or until the asparagus is tender. Cut into 1-inch diagonal lengths.

In a bowl beat the eggs, cream, milk, Parmesan cheese, nutmeg, and salt and black pepper to taste. Stir in the cooked asparagus lightly. Pour into the partially baked pie shell. Bake in the center of a preheated 375°F. oven for 30 minutes, or until the tart is lightly browned and puffed. *Serves 4 to 6.*

*L o m b a r d y*

# LEEK TART
### (Crostata di porri)

※ ※ ※

| | |
|---|---|
| 1 | **pound leeks** |
| 2 | **tablespoons olive oil** |
| 2 | **tablespoons butter** |
| 2 | **tablespoons flour** |
| 1¹/₄ | **cup milk** |
| ³/₄ | **cup grated Gruyère cheese** |
| 2 | **eggs, beaten** |
| | **Salt** |
| | **Freshly ground black pepper** |
| | **9-inch partially baked pie shell** |

Trim the root ends of the leeks. Cut lengthwise into halves and wash away the dirt that collects between the leaves. Cut leeks into ¹/₂-inch lengths. Heat the olive oil in a saucepan. Add the leeks, cover, and cook gently for 30 minutes, or until the leeks are very soft.

Prepare a béchamel sauce from the butter, flour, and milk (for directions see page 61). Remove from the heat and stir in the Gruyère cheese, the egg, and the leeks. Season with salt and black pepper. Pour into the partially baked pie shell. Bake in the center of a preheated 375°F. oven for 30 minutes, or until the tart is lightly browned and puffed. *Serves 4 to 6.*

*Liguria*

## SWISS CHARD TART
### (Crostata di bietole)

———— ❦ ❦ ❦ ————

Swiss chard and spinach tarts are made all over northern Italy. This version tastes particularly good, although the addition of currants may seem unusual.

2 pounds Swiss chard
2 tablespoons olive olive
1/4 pound fontina cheese, coarsely grated
1 egg
2 tablespoons dried currants
1/8 teaspoon freshly grated nutmeg
Salt
Freshly ground black pepper
9-inch partially baked pie shell

Wash the Swiss chard and cook in a covered saucepan over moderate heat for 5 minutes until tender. The water clinging to the leaves is sufficient to prevent scorching. Drain, squeeze dry, and coarsely chop. Heat the olive oil in a pan and cook the chopped Swiss chard for 2 minutes. Place in a bowl and add the fontina cheese, egg, currants, nutmeg, and salt and black pepper to taste. Blend well together. Pour into the partially baked pie shell. Bake in the center of a preheated 375°F. oven for 25 minutes. *Serves 4 to 6.*

## Gratins and Casseroles
*(Timballi, tortoni, polpettone, etc.)*

A gratin is literally the crust that is formed when a dish is browned in the oven or under a broiler. The gratins in this chapter consist of vegetables or combinations of vegetables, with or without a sauce, that are topped with bread crumbs or grated cheese and baked in the oven.

A casserole is a one-dish meal that can be made in advance. It usually includes pasta or rice, vegetables, and a sauce, and is baked in the oven.

Both gratins and casseroles may be prepared ahead of time and baked in the oven at the last minute. They make delicious and unusual main courses. Two or three dishes may be combined for one large dinner, to provide a variety of tastes and textures.

*A b r u z z i*

### EGGPLANT TIMBALE
*(Timballo di melanzane)*

Scamorza is a fresh cheese made in the Abruzzi and Campania; it is good for cooking. Mozzarella makes an excellent substitute.

2  eggplants, 1½ pounds altogether
   Salt
   Flour
½  cup olive oil, approximately
6  ounces scamorza or mozzarella cheese,
   thinly sliced
2  eggs, beaten
   Freshly ground black pepper

¼ cup freshly grated pecorino cheese

Trim the ends of the eggplant but do not peel. Cut into slices ⅛ inch thick. Sprinkle with salt and set in a colander for 1 hour to release the bitter juices. Wash off the salt and pat slices dry with paper towels. Dip slices into flour and quickly fry in hot oil until golden on both sides. Drain on paper towels. Arrange a layer of fried eggplant on the bottom of a shallow baking dish. Cover with slices of cheese, pour in a little beaten egg, and sprinkle with salt and black pepper. Repeat the layers until all the ingredients are used. Sprinkle the top with grated cheese. Bake in a preheated 350°F. oven for 30 minutes, or until the top is golden. *Serves 4.*

*Campania*

## ZUCCHINI PARMIGIANA
### (Zucchini alla parmigiana)

5 or 6 zucchini, about 1½ pounds altogether
　Flour
½ cup olive oil, approximately
2 cups Tomato Sauce (page 57)
½ pound mozzarella cheese, thinly sliced
1 cup freshly grated Parmesan cheese

Trim the ends of the zucchini and cut them into lengthwise slices about ⅛ inch thick. Dip into flour and fry in hot oil until golden on both sides. Drain on paper towels.

Arrange a layer of fried zucchini on the bottom of a shallow baking dish. Cover with some tomato sauce, top with slices of mozzarella cheese, and sprinkle with Parmesan cheese. Repeat the layers until all the ingredients are used, finishing with mozzarella and Parmesan cheeses. Bake in a preheated 375°F. oven for 25 to 30 minutes or until the top is golden and the sauce is bubbling. *Serves 4.*

*Campania*

# EGGPLANT, ZUCCHINI, AND POTATO PIE
### *(Tortino di verdure)*

—————— 🌿🌿🌿 ——————

Mixed vegetable and cheese casseroles are common all over southern Italy. This is a satisfying and delicious combination.

1   small eggplant, about 1/2 pound
    Salt
2   medium-size potatoes, peeled
2   small zucchini
1/2  cup olive oil, approximately
1/2  cup whole wheat bread crumbs
1/4  cup finely chopped fresh parsley
2   teaspoons fresh basil, or 1/2 teaspoon dried
1   large onion, peeled and thinly sliced
1/2  pound mozzarella cheese, thinly sliced
3   eggs, beaten
    Salt
    Freshly ground black pepper

Peel the eggplant and cut into slices 1/4 inch thick. Sprinkle with salt and set in a colander for 1 hour to release the bitter juices. Wash off the salt and pat slices dry with paper towels. Bring the potatoes to a boil in lightly salted boiling water and cook for 20 minutes, or until they are tender. Drain, cool, and cut into slices 1/8 inch thick. Trim the ends of the zucchini and cut lengthwise into thin slices. Heat ¼ cup olive oil in a large frying pan and quickly fry the eggplant on both sides until golden. Drain on paper towels. Add a tablespoon or two of oil to the same frying pan and quickly fry the zucchini on both sides until golden. Drain on paper towels. Add two more tablespoons of oil and cook the onion over moderate heat for 7 minutes, or until it is translucent. Combine the bread crumbs, parsley, and basil in a bowl and season with salt and black pepper.

Arrange the onions in the bottom of a well-oiled baking dish. Top with a few slices of mozzarella cheese and a little beaten egg. Sprinkle lightly with the bread crumb mixture and a few drops of the remaining olive oil. Cover with the potato slices, then more mozzarella cheese, beaten egg, bread-crumb mixture, and olive oil. Repeat the layers, using the zucchini slices instead of potatoes and then the eggplant slices, ending with the bread-crumb mixture. Dribble 1 or 2 tablespoons of olive oil over all. Bake in a preheated 350°F. oven for 30 to 40 minutes, until the top is golden. *Serves 4 to 6.*

*Liguria*

# GREEN BEAN AND POTATO PUDDING
### *(Polpettone di fagiolini e patate)*

Elsewhere in Italy *polpettone* means a croquette. In Liguria, *polpettone* is a vegetable purée mixed with eggs and sometimes ricotta cheese, and baked in a crust of butter and bread crumbs.

1 **pound green beans**
1 **pound potatoes**

4   eggs
1/2 cup freshly grated Parmesan cheese
2   tablespoons olive oil
2   garlic cloves, crushed
2   tablespoons finely chopped fresh parsley
2   tablespoons fresh marjoram, or 1/2
    teaspoon dried
    Salt
    Freshly ground black pepper
    Oil
1/2 cup whole wheat bread crumbs
2   tablespoons butter

Trim the ends of the green beans. Steam beans for 15 minutes, or until tender. Peel the potatoes and bring to a boil in lightly salted water; cook for 20 minutes, or until they are tender. Force the green beans and potatoes through a food mill, or purée in a blender, with a little liquid from the boiled potatoes. Blend in the eggs, one at a time, and stir in the Parmesan cheese. Heat the olive oil in a small frying pan and cook the garlic, parsley, and marjoram for 1 minute. Add the green bean mixture and season with salt and black pepper. Blend well.

Oil the bottom and sides of a large shallow baking dish. Dust with half of the bread crumbs. Turn baking dish over and shake out any excess crumbs. Pour in the green bean mixture, top with the remaining bread crumbs, and dot with butter. Bake in a preheated 350°F. oven for 45 to 50 minutes, or until the *polpettone* is nicely puffed and the top is golden. *Serves 4.*

*Liguria*

# POTATO, SPINACH, AND PEA PUDDING
## (Polpettone di patate, spinaci, e piselli)

Sometimes called *la torta verde* or "green pie."

| | |
|---|---|
| 1½ | cups shelled fresh peas |
| 2 | pounds potatoes |
| ½ | pound spinach |
| 4 | eggs, well beaten |
| ¾ | cup freshly grated Parmesan cheese |
| | Salt |
| | Freshly ground black pepper |
| ½ | cup whole wheat bread crumbs |
| ¼ | pound mozzarella cheese, thinly sliced |
| 2 | tablespoons butter |

Boil the peas for 15 to 30 minutes, until tender. The exact time will depend upon the age and size of the peas. Force through a food mill, or purée in a blender, and set aside. Peel the potatoes and bring to a boil in lightly salted water. Cook for 20 minutes, or until they are tender. Force through a food mill or potato ricer and set aside. Wash the spinach carefully and cook in a covered saucepan over moderate heat for 5 minutes. The water clinging to the leaves is sufficient to prevent scorching. Drain, squeeze dry, and chop coarsely. Combine the pea, potato, and chopped spinach purées in a large bowl, and add the eggs one at a time. Stir in the grated cheese, salt and black pepper to taste and blend well.

Oil the bottom and sides of a large, shallow baking dish and sprinkle with half of the bread crumbs. Turn baking dish over and shake out any excess crumbs. Pour in half the potato mixture. Cover with slices of mozzarella cheese. Pour in remaining potato mixture, sprinkle with remaining bread crumbs, and dot with butter. Bake in a preheated 350°F. oven for 45 to 50 minutes, or until the pudding is nicely puffed and the top is golden. *Serves 4 to 6.*

*A p u l i a*

# TIELLA
## (Tiella)

꧁ ꧁ ꧁

*Tiella* is a distant relative of the Spanish rice dish—*paella*—and it dates back to the days when southern Italy was under Spanish rule. One of the main differences is that *tiella* is based on potatoes, one of Apulia's favorite vegetables. Sometimes both potatoes and rice are used. The rest of the ingredients vary from town to town.

⅓   cup olive oil
2   garlic cloves, crushed
1   handful of parsley, finely chopped
2   teaspoons fresh basil, or ½ teaspoon dried
2   large onions, thinly sliced
½   pound mushrooms, thinly sliced
    Salt
    Freshly ground black pepper
2   pounds waxy potatoes
6   ounces mozzarella cheese, thinly sliced
½   cup freshly grated Parmesan cheese
½   cup whole wheat bread crumbs

Heat half of the olive oil in a large frying pan and cook the garlic, parsley, basil, and onions over moderate heat for 3 minutes. Add the mushrooms and continue to cook for another 5 minutes, or until the mushrooms are tender. Season with salt and black pepper and set aside.

Peel the potatoes and bring to a boil in lightly salted boiling water. Cook for 10 to 12 minutes, or until they are just tender. Let cool slightly and slice thinly.

Oil a large shallow baking dish and spread half of the onions and mushrooms over the bottom. Cover with half of the potato slices and sprinkle with salt and black pepper. Top with half of the mozzarella slices and sprinkle with Parmesan cheese. Repeat the layers, ending with mozzarella and Parmesan cheeses. Sprinkle the bread crumbs over the top and dribble remaining olive oil over the bread crumbs. Bake in a preheated 375°F. oven for 30 to 40 minutes, or until the top is golden. *Serves 4 to 6.*

*Lombardy*

## CAULIFLOWER AND RICE CASSEROLE

### (Crostata di riso e cavolfiore)

1 medium-size cauliflower
1 tablespoon olive oil
1 small onion, finely chopped
1 teaspoon finely chopped parsley
1 cup raw rice
2 cups Vegetable Broth (page 69) or water, boiling
1/2 teaspoon salt
2 tablespoons butter
1/3 cup freshly grated Parmesan cheese
1 1/2 cups Béchamel Sauce (page 61)

⅓  cup grated Gruyère cheese

Cut away the stem of the cauliflower and break the head into flowerets. Steam flowerets for 8 minutes, or until they are tender.

Heat the olive oil in a small saucepan and cook the onion and parsley over moderate heat for 3 minutes. Stir in the rice and cook for 1 minute so each grain is coated with oil. Add the boiling broth and ½ teaspoon salt. Cover and cook gently for 8 to 10 minutes, until the rice is tender but still firm. Remove from the heat and stir in the butter and ¼ cup Parmesan cheese. Prepare the béchamel sauce. Remove from the heat and stir in the Gruyère cheese.

Spread a layer of rice in the bottom of a well-buttered, shallow baking dish. Spoon a little of the cheese sauce over the rice. Cover with a layer of cauliflower. Repeat the layers, ending with the cheese sauce. Sprinkle the top with the remaining grated Parmesan cheese. Bake in a preheated 375°F. oven for 20 to 25 minutes, or until the top is golden. *Serves 4 to 6.*

*Emilia - Romagna and the North*

## BROCCOLI GRATIN
*(Broccoli gratinati)*

1  large bunch of broccoli, about 2 pounds
2  cups Béchamel Sauce (page 61)
⅓  cup freshly grated Parmesan cheese
2  tablespoons whole wheat bread crumbs or wheat germ
2  tablespoons butter

Trim the stem ends of the broccoli. Break heads into flowerets and cut stems into bite-size pieces. Steam for 8 minutes, or until it is just tender.

Prepare the béchamel sauce. Remove from heat and stir in ¼ cup of the grated cheese. Pour some of the sauce into the bottom of a shallow baking dish. Cover with broccoli and pour remaining sauce over the vegetable.

Mix the bread crumbs with the remaining grated cheese and sprinkle over the top of the sauce. Dot with butter. Bake in a preheated 375°F. oven for 25 to 30 minutes, or until the top is golden. *Serves 4.*

*Valle d'Aosta*

## POTATO PIE
### *(Tortino di patate)*

――――― ❦❦❦ ―――――

    3  pounds potatoes, peeled and thinly sliced
    1  large onion, thinly sliced
 1½  cups grated Gruyère cheese
    ½  cup freshly grated Parmesan cheese
    2  cups milk, or half milk and half vegetable
        broth
    ¼  teaspoon freshly grated nutmeg
        Salt
        Freshly ground black pepper
    2  tablespoons butter

Butter a large baking dish and arrange half of the potatoes on the bottom. Cover with half of the onion, then half of the Gruyère cheese. Sprinkle with half of the Parmesan cheese. Repeat with remaining potatoes, onion, and Gruyère cheese. Bring the milk to just below a simmer. Add nutmeg, salt and black pepper to taste. Pour into the baking dish. Sprinkle the top with remaining Parmesan cheese and dot with butter. Cover loosely with aluminum foil. Bake in a preheated 350°F. oven for 25 minutes. Remove the foil and bake for 40 to 45 minutes longer, or until potatoes are tender and the top is golden. *Serves 4 to 6.*

## Fritters and Croquettes
*(Bignè e crocchette)*

Italians love fritters and croquettes. Most regions of Italy make a *Fritto Misto* or "Mixed Fry." A wide variety of ingredients are used, such as eggplant, zucchini, potato or rice, ricotta cheese, or fried artichokes. They make a delicious light supper served with a green salad on the side.

A light vegetable oil such as peanut or corn oil is best for deep-frying. Safflower or sunflower seed oil are unsuitable for deep-frying. The oil should be heated to about 360°F. before the fritters are added. To test for the correct heat, drop a morsel of bread into the hot oil. When it turns golden the oil is ready to be used.

Do not overcrowd the fritters when cooking. Leave plenty of room for them to puff out. The first batch of fritters may be kept warm in a preheated 325°F. oven while the next batch is cooking.

### FRITTER BATTER
*(Pastella per bignè)*

❧❧❧

1/2  cup whole-wheat or unbleached white
     flour
1/4  teaspoon salt
 3   eggs
3/4  cup milk

Mix the flour, salt, and eggs well together in a bowl. Gradually stir in the milk to form a smooth batter with the consistency of heavy cream. Refrigerate for 2 hours before using. *Makes about 1½ cups.*

*Umbria*

## CARDOON FRITTERS, PERUGIA STYLE
### *(Cardi alla perugina)*

Cardoons are members of the thistle family. The long fleshy stalks and ribs, which are similar to celery, are the parts used. Like artichokes, they should be dropped into acidulated water or rubbed with lemon juice when cut, to prevent them discoloring.

1½  pounds cardoons
     Juice of 1 lemon
  2  cups Fritter Batter (page 176)
     Oil for deep-frying
  2  cups Mushroom and Tomato Sauce (page 60)
 ½  pound mozzarella cheese, thinly sliced
 ½  cup freshly grated Parmesan cheese

Trim the outer ribs of the cardoons and remove any stringy parts as you would for celery. Cut remaining stalks into 2-inch lengths and drop into acidulated water (juice of 1 lemon to 1 quart water). Steam for about 1½ hours, or until cardoons are tender. Dip into the frying batter and fry in hot (375°F.) oil until golden on both sides. Drain on paper towels.

Prepare the mushroom and tomato sauce and spoon a layer of the sauce into the bottom of a well-oiled baking dish. Cover with a layer of cardoon fritters. Top with slices of mozzarella cheese and sprinkle with Parmesan cheese. Bake in a preheated 400°F. oven for 20 minutes, or until the top is golden. *Serves 4 to 6.*

*Apulia*

# EGGPLANT AND MOZZARELLA FRITTERS
### (Fritto di melanzane filanti)

2  medium-size eggplants, about 1½ pounds
   altogether
   Salt
1  cup ricotta cheese
1  cup small dice of mozzarella cheese
½  cup freshly grated Parmesan cheese
1  tablespoon finely chopped fresh parsley
1  egg yolk
   Freshly ground black pepper
2  cups Fritter Batter (page 176)
   Oil for deep-frying

Peel the eggplants and cut into crosswise slices, ⅛ inch thick. Sprinkle with salt, set in a colander, and leave for 1 hour to release the bitter juices. Wash off the salt and pat slices dry with paper towels.

In a bowl combine the ricotta, mozzarella, and Parmesan cheeses, the parsley, egg yolk, and salt and black pepper to taste and blend well. Sandwich a little of this filling between 2 slices of eggplant. Dip into the fritter batter and press the edges firmly together with a fork. Fry in 375°F. oil until golden on both sides. Drain on paper towels and serve at once. *Serves 6.*

*Lazio*

## Ricotta Cheese Fritters
### *(Doratini di ricotta)*

These crisp, light fritters are simple to prepare. They are perfect with cocktails, as an antipasto, or can serve for a light lunch or supper dish.

2   cups ricotta cheese
2   eggs
1/2  cup freshly grated Parmesan cheese
1/4  cup flour
     Salt
     Freshly ground black pepper
1/8  teaspoon freshly grated nutmeg
     Flour
     Oil for deep-frying

In a bowl combine the ricotta cheese, eggs, grated cheese, and flour. Add salt and black pepper to taste and the nutmeg and blend well together. Form into small balls the size of a walnut. Roll in flour and fry in 375°F. oil until golden on both sides. Drain on paper towels and serve at once. *Serves 4.*

*All Italy*

# MIXED FRY
### *(Fritto misto)*

Each region of Italy makes its own combination of mixed fry. I have selected a typical vegetable combination, but you may include any of the following: artichoke hearts, asparagus tips, beets, broccoli, cardoons, celery, eggplant, scorzonera (oyster plant), or green tomatoes.

1½   cups whole-wheat or unbleached white
      flour
½    teaspoon salt
2    eggs, separated
2    tablespoons olive oil
2    tablespoons brandy
1    cup water, approximately
½    bunch of broccoli
1    fennel bulb, trimmed and cut into strips
2    small zucchini
½    pound button mushrooms
      Oil for deep-frying
1    lemon, cut into wedges

Combine the flour and salt in a bowl and make a well in the center. Add the egg yolks, olive oil, and brandy. Stir in enough of the water to form a smooth batter. Let stand for 1 hour.

Trim the stems of the broccoli and cut into sections. Steam with the fennel strips for 8 to 10 minutes, until both vegetables are just tender. Meanwhile trim the ends of the zucchini and cut into quarters lengthwise. Wash the mushrooms and pat dry.

Beat the egg whites stiff and fold into the batter. Dip all the vegetables into the batter and fry in 375°F. oil until golden on both sides. Do not overcrowd while frying or the fritters will not be crisp. Drain on paper towels. When all the fritters are cooked, serve at once with lemon wedges. *Serves 6.*

*Campania*

## EGGPLANT FRITTERS
### (Bignè di melanzane)

❦ ❦ ❦

Eggplant fritters are so delicious that I have included another simpler version.

2   medium-size eggplant, about 1½ pounds
     altogether
     Salt
2   cups Fritter Batter (page 176)
     Oil for deep-frying

Peel the eggplant and cut into slices about ½ inch thick. Sprinkle with salt and set in a colander for 1 hour to release the bitter juices. Wash off the salt and pat slices dry.

Dip the slices into the fritter batter and fry in 375°F. oil until golden on both sides. Drain on paper towels and serve at once. *Serves 4 to 6.*

*Friuli, Venezia Giulia*

# FENNEL FRITTERS
### (Fritole di fenoci)

4   fennel bulbs
<br>½  cup Vinaigrette Sauce (page 65)
<br>2   cups Fritter Batter (page 176)
<br>    Oil for deep-frying

Remove the coarse outer leaves and the stems from the fennel bulbs. Trim the bases and cut into wedges. Steam the wedges for 20 to 30 minutes, or until they are just tender. Transfer to a bowl and pour vinaigrette sauce over them. Leave to marinate for 1 hour.

Dip the fennel wedges into the batter and fry in 375°F. oil until golden on both sides. Drain on paper towels and serve at once. *Serves 4.*

*Trentino*

# BEAN PATTIES
### (Polpettine di fagioli)

2   cups cooked dried white beans
<br>2   tablespoons minced onion
<br>1   egg
<br>2   tablespoons freshly grated Parmesan cheese
<br>    Pinch of cloves
<br>    Salt

**Freshly ground black pepper**
¹/₂ **cup wheat germ, approximately**
**Oil for deep frying**

Force the beans through a sieve into a mixing bowl, or purée in a food processor. Add the onion, egg, Parmesan cheese, cloves, and salt and black pepper to taste. Stir in ¹/₄ cup wheat germ and blend well. The mixture should be firm enough to hold a shape. If the mixture is too soft, add a little more wheat germ. Form into patties about 2 inches in diameter and ¹/₂ inch thick. Coat with wheat germ and fry in hot (360°F.) oil until golden on both sides. *Serves 4.*

*Valle d'Aosta*

## POTATO PANCAKE
### *(Fritelle di patate)*

A children's favorite.

1 **pound potatoes**
2 **tablespoons whole-wheat or unbleached white flour**
¹/₄ **cup freshly grated Parmesan cheese**
1 **egg**
1 **handful of parsley, finely chopped**
2 **tablespoons fresh basil**
**Salt**
**Freshly ground black pepper**
3 **tablespoons olive oil**

Peel the potatoes and grate on a coarse grater into a mixing bowl.

Add the whole-wheat flour, Parmesan cheese, egg, parsley, basil, and season with salt and black pepper. Mix well.

Heat the olive oil in a large frying pan with a flameproof handle. Put in the potato mixture and spread out evenly in one layer. Cook gently for 15 minutes until the bottom is nicely browned.

Turn on the broiler to high. Set the frying pan in the lower third of the broiler so the frying pan is about 12 inches away from the source of heat. Broil for 8 to 10 minutes, until the top of the pancake is golden. Serve at once. *Serves 2 to 3.*

*Lazio*

## STUFFED POTATO CROQUETTES
### *(Crocchette di patate con mozzarella)*

—————— 🌿🌿🌿 ——————

A specialty of Naples.

1½   pounds potatoes, peeled
3    eggs
½    cup whole wheat flour
¼    cup freshly grated Parmesan cheese
⅛    teaspoon freshly grated nutmeg
     Salt
     Freshly ground black pepper
1    cup mozzarella cheese, cut into small cubes
     Flour for dusting
     Bread crumbs
     Oil for deep frying

Boil the potatoes in lightly salted water for 20 minutes, or until they are tender. Drain and sieve, or put through a potato ricer into a mixing bowl. Add 1 egg and blend well together. Stir in the whole wheat flour, Parmesan cheese, nutmeg, and salt and black pepper to taste. Form into small balls the size of a lime. Punch a deep hole in each one with the forefinger and push a cube of mozzarella into the center. Cover with a little potato mixture so the filling is completely encased. Roll in flour, dip in the remaining eggs, beaten, then roll in bread crumbs. Fry in hot (375°F.) oil until golden on both sides. *Serves 4.*

*L a z i o*

## RICE CROQUETTES WITH CHEESE AND MUSHROOMS
### (Suppli al telefono con funghi)

In Rome *suppli* are made with provatura cheese that is made from buffalo's milk. Mozzarella makes a perfect substitute. They are called telephone croquettes because the hot melted cheese hangs like a telephone wire around your face when you bite into them.

   2  tablespoons olive oil
   1  garlic clove, crushed
   1  handful of parsley, finely chopped
      Few leaves of fresh mint, or ⅛ teaspoon dried
  ½  pound mushrooms, chopped
  3  cups cooked rice
  2  eggs
      Salt
      Freshly ground black pepper
  ⅓  cup small cubes of mozzarella cheese
      Whole-wheat flour
      Bread crumbs
      Oil for deep-frying

Heat the olive oil in a frying pan and cook the garlic, parsley, and mint for 1 minute. Add the mushrooms and cook over moderate heat for 5 minutes. Set aside to cool slightly.

Place the cooked rice in a mixing bowl and add 1 egg and salt and black pepper to taste. Mix well. Moisten your hands with cold water and shape the rice into balls the size of a lemon. With your forefinger punch a hole into the center. Place a teaspoon of the mushroom mixture and a cube of mozzarella into each hole. Cover the cheese with rice, so it is completely enclosed. Roll in whole-wheat flour, dip in the remaining egg, beaten, then roll in bread crumbs. Fry in hot (360°F.) oil until crisp and golden. *Serves 4 to 6.*

*Apulia*

## ZUCCHINI CROQUETTES
### *(Polpettone di zucchini)*

|   |   |
|---|---|
| 3 | medium-size potatoes |
| 1 | egg, beaten |
| 2 | zucchini, coarsely grated |
| 1 | large onion, grated |
| 3/4 | cup freshly grated Parmesan cheese |
| 1 | slice of whole-wheat bread, about 1 inch thick |
| 1/2 | cup milk |
| 1/4 | teaspoon freshly grated nutmeg |
|   | Salt |
|   | Freshly ground black pepper |
|   | Oil for deep-frying |

Boil the potatoes in lightly salted water for 20 minutes, or until they are tender. Drain and press through a sieve into a mixing bowl. Add the beaten egg, grated zucchini, onion, and Parmesan cheese and blend well. Remove the crusts from the slice of bread and soak bread in the milk. Squeeze dry and add to the potato mixture. Season with nutmeg, and salt and black pepper to taste. Form into balls the size of a lime and fry in hot (375°F.) oil until golden on both sides. *Serves 4.*

## Stuffed Vegetables
### *(Legumi imbottite)*

Italians love stuffed vegetables. Eggplants, zucchini, sweet peppers, onions, mushrooms, and tomatoes are the most usual vegetables to stuff. There are probably as many different versions of each as there are cooks.

Stuffed vegetables make an excellent main course, but if you use smaller quantities, they may also be used as an appetizer or a vegetable accompaniment.

*Liguria*

### STUFFED ZUCCHINI WITH MUSHROOMS
### *(Zucchini ripieni)*

The zucchini are filled with a delicate stuffing of onions, mushrooms, herbs, and grated cheese. Sometimes dried mushrooms are used instead.

6   medium-size zucchini
2   tablespoons olive oil
1   garlic clove, crushed

1    handful of parsley, chopped
1    tablespoon fresh marjoram, or $\frac{1}{2}$ teaspoon
      dried
1    small onion, finely chopped
$\frac{1}{4}$   pound mushrooms, chopped
$\frac{3}{4}$   cup whole-wheat bread crumbs, soaked in
      $\frac{1}{4}$ cup milk
$\frac{2}{3}$   cup freshly grated Parmesan cheese
1    egg, beaten
      Salt
      Freshly ground black pepper
2    tablespoons butter

Steam the zucchini for 10 minutes, or until they are just tender. Cool slightly. Cut lengthwise into halves and scoop out the flesh with an apple corer, leaving shells $\frac{1}{4}$ inch thick. Chop the portions you scooped out.

Heat the olive oil in a frying pan and cook the garlic, parsley, and marjoram for 1 minute. Add the onion and cook over moderate heat for 5 minutes. Add the chopped zucchini and mushrooms and continue to cook until the vegetables are tender and turning golden. Place the onion mixture, the bread crumbs soaked in milk, half of the Parmesan cheese, the egg, and salt and black pepper to taste in a bowl and mix well together.

Stuff the zucchini shells with the mixture. Sprinkle with remaining grated cheese and dot with butter. Arrange side by side on a well-oiled baking sheet. Bake in a preheated 350°F. oven for 30 minutes, or until the tops are golden. *Serves 3.*

*Tuscany*

# Stuffed Zucchini Florentine
*(Zucchini ripieni alla fiorentina)*

This is an elegant dish, perfect for a dinner party. The zucchini are stuffed with a mixture of spinach, herbs, and cheese, topped with a béchamel sauce and grated cheese, and baked in the oven until the tops are golden. The dish may be prepared ahead of time and baked in the oven just before serving.

| | |
|---|---|
| 8 | small zucchini |
| 1/2 | pound spinach |
| 2 | tablespoons olive oil |
| 1 | garlic clove, crushed |
| 2 | tablespoons chopped parsley |
| 1 | cup freshly grated Parmesan cheese |
| 1/8 | teaspoon freshly grated nutmeg |
| | Salt |
| | Freshly ground black pepper |
| 2 | cups Béchamel Sauce (page 61) |

Steam the zucchini for 10 minutes, or until they are just tender. Cool slightly. Cut lengthwise into halves and scoop out the flesh with an apple corer, leaving a shell 1/4 inch thick. Chop the portions you scooped out.

Wash the spinach carefully and cook in a covered saucepan over moderate heat for 5 minutes. The water clinging to the leaves is sufficient to prevent scorching. Drain and coarsely chop.

Heat the olive oil in a frying pan and cook the garlic and parsley for 1 minute. Add the chopped zucchini and cook over moderately high heat for 5 minutes, or until the zucchini are tender and turning golden. Add the chopped spinach, ¼ cup of the Parmesan cheese, the nutmeg, and salt and black pepper to taste.

Spoon the mixture into the zucchini halves and place side by side in a well-oiled shallow baking dish. Prepare the béchamel sauce. Remove from the heat and stir in ½ cup of the grated Parmesan cheese. Pour sauce over the stuffed zucchini. Sprinkle with remaining grated cheese. Bake in a preheated 400°F. oven for 20 to 25 minutes, or until the tops are golden. *Serves 4.*

*Campania*

## STUFFED EGGPLANT WITH ALMONDS
### (Melanzane imbottite con mandorle)

| | |
|---|---|
| 3 | small eggplants, about ½ pound each |
| ¼ | cup olive oil |
| 1 | garlic clove, crushed |
| 1 | onion, chopped |
| 1 | handful fresh parsley, finely chopped |
| 2 | teaspoons fresh oregano, or ½ teaspoon dried |
| 3 | or 4 plum tomatoes, peeled, seeded, and chopped |
| ¼ | cup shelled almonds, finely ground in the blender |
| ¼ | cup whole-wheat bread crumbs |
| | Salt |
| | Freshly ground black pepper |
| ⅓ | cup freshly grated Parmesan cheese |

Place the eggplants in a saucepan of boiling water. Cover and simmer for 5 minutes. Remove. Cut lengthwise into halves. Scoop out the pulp, taking care not to damage the skins, leaving a shell ⅛ inch thick. Chop the pulp coarsely.

Heat the olive oil in a frying pan and cook the garlic, onion, parsley, and oregano over moderate heat for 3 minutes. Add the chopped eggplant and tomatoes. Cover and simmer for 10 to 15 minutes, or until the eggplant is tender.

Remove from heat and stir in the ground almonds, bread crumbs, and salt and black pepper to taste. Fill the eggplant shells with the mixture and sprinkle the grated cheese on top.

Place side by side on a well-oiled shallow baking dish. Bake in a preheated 350°F. oven for 30 minutes, or until the tops are nicely browned. *Serves 4 to 6.*

*All Italy*

# PEPPERS STUFFED WITH RICE AND PINE NUTS
*(Peperoni imbottite di riso)*

Stuffed peppers are made all over Italy. This recipe has a simple rice stuffing flavored with tomato sauce, herbs, and pine nuts, which give it a delicious nutty flavor.

6   to 8 red or green sweet peppers
¼   cup olive oil
1   small onion, chopped
1   tablespoon chopped fresh basil, or ¼
     teaspoon dried
2   tablespoons finely chopped fresh parsley

1   cup raw rice
2½   cups Vegetable Broth (page 69), boiling
2   cups Tomato Sauce (page 57)
¼   cup pine nuts
½   cup freshly grated Parmesan cheese
    Salt
    Freshly ground black pepper

Wash the sweet peppers and place in a saucepan of boiling water. Cover, and simmer for 5 minutes. Cut in half lengthwise and remove the seeds and pith. Heat 2 tablespoons of olive oil in a saucepan and cook the onion, basil, and parsley for 3 minutes. Stir in the rice and cook for 1 minute. Add 2 cups of the broth, cover, and simmer for 15 to 20 minutes, until ¾ cooked.

Drain and transfer to a mixing bowl. Stir in ½ cup tomato sauce, the pine nuts, ¼ cup Parmesan cheese, and salt and black pepper to taste. Stuff the pepper halves with the mixture. Sprinkle the remaining Parmesan cheese over the top and dribble over the remaining olive oil.

Arrange peppers side by side in a well-oiled shallow baking dish. Pour the remaining tomato sauce, mixed with the remaining ½ cup of broth around the sweet peppers. Bake in a preheated 350°F. oven for 50 minutes, or until the tops are golden and the rice is cooked. *Serves 4 to 6.*

*Sicily*

## SICILIAN STUFFED PEPPERS
*(Peperoni imbottite alla siciliana)*

Stuffed peppers are versatile; they may be served as an antipasto or light main course, and are especially good for a buffet, as they can be served hot or at room temperature. The sweet-and-sour combination of white raisins, pine nuts, olives, and capers is typical of Sicilian cooking.

|       |                                               |
|-------|-----------------------------------------------|
| 6     | green or red sweet peppers                    |
| 1½    | cups whole-wheat bread crumbs                 |
| 3     | tablespoons pine nuts                         |
| 3     | tablespoons white raisins                     |
| 2     | tablespoons capers                            |
| ¼     | cup Italian or Greek black olives, pitted and chopped |
| ½     | cup olive oil                                 |
| ¼     | cup finely chopped fresh parsley              |
| 2     | teaspoons fresh basil, or ½ teaspoon dried    |
|       | Salt                                          |
|       | Freshly ground black pepper                   |
| 2     | cups Tomato Sauce (page 57)                   |
| ½     | cup boiling water                             |

Wash the sweet peppers, cut lengthwise into halves, and remove the seeds and ribs. In a bowl combine the bread crumbs, pine nuts, white raisins, capers, olives, and olive oil, parsley, basil, and salt and black pepper to taste, and blend well together. Stuff the peppers with the mixture and arrange side by side in a well-oiled shallow baking dish. Pour the tomato sauce, mixed with the boiling water, around the peppers. Bake in a preheated 350°F. oven for 50 to 60 minutes, until the tops are golden. If the tomato sauce becomes too dry, add a little more water. *Serves 4 to 6.*

*Emilia-Romagna and the North*

## STUFFED MUSHROOM CAPS
*(Funghi imbottite)*

 24 large mushroom caps
 1/2 cup olive oil, approximately
 2 garlic cloves, crushed
 1 small onion, finely chopped
 1 handful of parsley, finely chopped
 1 teaspoon fresh oregano, or 1/4 teaspoon
  dried
  Pinch of dried thyme
 1 cup whole-wheat bread crumbs
 1/3 cup freshly grated Parmesan cheese
 1/8 teaspoon freshly grated nutmeg
  Salt
  Freshly ground black pepper

Wash the mushrooms, remove the stems, and arrange the caps side by side in a well-oiled shallow baking dish. Chop the stems finely and set aside. Heat 1/4 cup olive oil in a frying pan and cook the garlic, onion, mushroom stems, parsley, oregano, and thyme over moderate heat for 5 minutes. Remove from the heat and stir in the bread crumbs, Parmesan cheese, nutmeg, and salt and black pepper to taste. Stuff the mushroom caps with the mixture and sprinkle with remaining olive oil. Bake in a preheated 350°F. oven for 20 minutes, or until the tops are golden. *Serves 4 to 6.*

*Liguria*

## STUFFED TOMATOES
### (Pomodori al forno)

4   large firm tomatoes
½   pound Swiss chard or spinach
¾   cup ricotta cheese
1   egg
¼   cup freshly grated Parmesan cheese
1   handful parsley, finely chopped
1   teaspoon fresh marjoram, or ¼ teaspoon
    dried
3   tablespoons olive oil
    Salt
    Freshly ground black pepper
¼   cup whole-wheat bread crumbs

Cut the tomatoes crosswise into halves and scoop out most of the pulp and seeds, leaving a shell about ¼ inch thick.

Wash the Swiss chard and cook in a covered saucepan over moderate heat for 6 minutes. The water clinging to the leaves is sufficient to prevent scorching. Drain, squeeze dry, and chop finely. In a bowl combine the ricotta cheese, egg, Parmesan cheese, Swiss chard, parsley, marjoram, and 1 teaspoon of olive oil and blend well together. Season with salt and black pepper. Stuff the tomato halves with the mixture. Sprinkle the tops with bread crumbs and dribble remaining olive oil over the tops. Arrange in a well-oiled baking dish. Bake for 30 to 35 minutes, or until the tops are golden and the tomatoes are tender but still retain their shape. *Serves 2 to 4.*

## Crêpes
### (Crespelle)

Crêpes make delicious versatile main courses. They may be filled
with vegetables of all kinds or any of the fillings for stuffed pasta,
then topped with sauce and browned under the broiler or in a hot
oven.

Crêpe batter should be made at least 2 hours before cooking.
The batter will need to be mixed again before using. If it has thickened, a little more water should be added to give it the consistency
of thin cream.

A heavy cast-iron pan with sloping sides, 5 to 6 inches in diameter, is best for crrêpes. To keep cooked crêpes warm, place them
in the bowl of a soup plate, cover with an inverted soup plate, and
set the plates on top of a saucepan of simmering water. Crêpes can
be stored in the refrigerator for up to 2 days or frozen for up to 2
months if well wrapped.

*All Italy*

## CRÊPE BATTER
### (Pasta per crespelle)

❦ ❦ ❦

1½  cups whole-wheat or unbleached white
    flour
 3  eggs
    Pinch of salt
1¾  cups water, or half milk and half water
 2  tablespoons olive oil

Place the flour in a bowl. Make a well in the center and drop in the
eggs and salt. Mix well with a wooden spoon. Gradually add the
water, beating constantly to form a smooth batter with the consis-

tency of thin cream. Let batter stand for at least 2 hours before using.

Heat a little olive oil in a 6-inch heavy frying pan. When it is hot, pour in 2½ to 3 tablespoons of batter. Quickly tilt the pan in all directions so the batter evenly covers the pan. Cook for about 1 minute on each side. Slide onto a soup plate as described in previous recipe to keep them warm. Lightly oil the pan again and repeat until the batter is used. *Makes 15 crêpes.*

*A b r u z z i*

## STUFFED PANCAKES WITH PEAS
### (Scrippelle 'mbusse)

There are many versions of *scrippelle 'mbusse* in the Abruzzi. The stuffing and sauce may vary but peas are always included.

15 crêpes
2 cups shelled young tender peas
1 cup Béchamel Sauce (page 61)
1 cup freshly grated Parmesan cheese
2 cups Mushroom and Tomato Sauce (page 60)

Make the crêpes from the batter on page 196. Cook the peas in a little water for 10 to 12 minutes, or until they are tender. The exact time will depend on the size and age of the peas. Prepare the béchamel sauce. Stir in ⅓ cup Parmesan cheese and the peas. Spoon a little of this filling into each crêpe and roll up. Arrange crêpes in a single layer in a well-oiled shallow baking dish. Cover with the mushroom and tomato sauce. Bake in a preheated 375°F.

oven until crêpes are heated through. Just before serving, sprinkle with a little grated cheese. Serve with remaining grated cheese on the side. *Serves 4 or 5.*

*Emilia-Romagna*

## ZUCCHINI-FILLED CRÊPES
*(Crespelle imbottite con zucchini)*

———— 🌿🌿🌿 ————

This is a simple but elegant main course. Mushrooms make a good variation.

15  crêpes
3  small zucchini
3  tablespoons olive oil
1¹/₂  cups Béchamel Sauce (page 61)
²/₃  cup freshly grated Parmesan cheese
1  cup Vegetable Broth (page 69), hot
3  tablespoons butter, melted

Make the crêpes from the batter on page 196. Trim the ends of the zucchini and cut the vegetables into thin slices. Heat the olive oil in a large frying pan and quickly fry the zucchini until slices are golden on both sides. Drain on paper towels.

Prepare the béchamel sauce. Stir in half of the Parmesan cheese and the fried zucchini. Spoon a little of this filling into the center of each crêpe, and roll up.

Arrange crêpes in a single layer in a well-oiled shallow baking dish. Pour in the hot broth. Sprinkle with remaining Parmesan cheese and dribble the melted butter over all. Bake in a preheated 375°F. oven for 15 minutes, or until crêpes are heated through and the broth, Parmesan cheese, and butter have combined to make a light sauce. *Serves 4 or 5.*

*Campania*

## CRÊPES WITH CHEESE AND PARSLEY FILLING
*(Crespelle imbottite con ricotta)*

15  crêpes
1   cup ricotta cheese
2   eggs
¹/₂ pound mozzarella cheese, cut into small dice
1   cup freshly grated Parmesan cheese
1   handful of parsley, finely chopped
    Salt
    Freshly ground black pepper
2   cups Tomato Sauce (page 57)

Make the crêpes from the batter on page 196. In a bowl combine the ricotta cheese, eggs, mozzarella, ¹/₂ cup of the Parmesan cheese, the parsley, and salt and black pepper to taste, and blend well together. Spoon a little of this filling into the center of each crêpe, and roll up.

Arrange crêpes in a single layer in a well-oiled shallow baking dish. Pour the tomato sauce over all. Bake in a preheated 375°F. oven for 15 minutes, or until crêpes and sauce are heated through. Just before serving, sprinkle with a little grated cheese. Serve with remaining grated cheese on the side. *Serves 4 to 6.*

*Emilia - Romagna*

## SPINACH, CHEESE, AND TOMATO CRÊPE CAKE
### *(Timballo di crespelle)*

12  crêpes
1½  pounds spinach
¼  cup heavy cream
⅛  teaspoon freshly grated nutmeg
    Salt
    Freshly ground black pepper
1½  cups Béchamel Sauce (page 61)
½  cup grated Gruyère cheese
1½  cups ricotta cheese
1  egg
2  tablespoons milk
1½  cups Tomato Sauce (page 57)
½  cup freshly grated Parmesan cheese

Make the crêpes from the batter on page 196. Wash the spinach and cook in a covered saucepan over moderate heat for 5 minutes. Drain and chop coarsely. Combine in a bowl with the heavy cream, nutmeg, and salt and black pepper to taste. Prepare the béchamel sauce and remove from the heat. Stir in the Gruyère cheese.

Combine the ricotta cheese, egg, and milk in a bowl and beat until smooth.

Arrange a crêpe in the bottom of a well-buttered 2-quart soufflé dish. Spoon a third of the spinach mixture over the crêpe and sprinkle with a little Parmesan cheese. Cover with another crêpe and spoon a third of cheese sauce over it. Cover with another crêpe and spoon a third of the ricotta mixture over it. Top with another crêpe and spoon a third of the tomato sauce over it. Repeat the layers until all the ingredients are used. Top with tomato sauce and grated cheese. Bake in a preheated 350°F. oven for 30 to 40 minutes, or until the top is golden and the sauce is bubbling. Serve cut into wedges like a cake. *Serves 6.*

# EGGS

☙☙☙

## UOVA

## *Frittatas*

*(Frittate)*

The Italian *frittata* is similar to the Spanish omelet. It is flat and
round and cooked on both sides like a pancake. It should not be
creamy like a French omelet, but firm and set.

Almost any cooked vegetable can be incorporated into a *frittata*,
together with grated cheese and herbs. Some *frittate* are thickened
slightly with bread crumbs or flour. Some are baked in the oven
like a pie.

To cook a *frittata*, heat a little olive oil in a heavy-bottomed frying
pan with a flameproof handle. Add the egg mixture and cook until
the bottom is nicely browned. Place the pan under a broiler for 20
seconds to set the top, then slide the *frittata* onto a saucepan lid or
plate. Place the frying pan over the uncooked side of the frittata
and hold it snugly against the saucepan lid. Quickly flip the saucepan lid over so the uncooked side of the *frittata* is on the bottom
of the frying pan. Continue cooking the *frittata* on top of the stove
until the bottom is golden. Slide it onto a serving platter. Serve cut
into wedges like a pie.

*Friuli and Venezia Giulia*

## LEEK, FENNEL, AND PEA FRITTATA
### *(Fertae cui cesarons)*

*Fertae cui cesarons* means "Frittata with peas."

> 2   tablespoons olive oil
> 1   onion, chopped
> 1   leek, cut into thin slices
> 1   fennel bulb, trimmed and cut into strips
> 1   teaspoon fresh mint, or ¼ teaspoon dried
> 1   cup shelled fresh peas
> 4   eggs
> ¼   teaspoon salt
>     A grinding of fresh black pepper
> 2   tablespoons butter

Heat the olive oil in a heavy frying pan and cook the onion, leek, fennel, and mint over moderate heat for 5 minutes. Add the peas and 2 or 3 tablespoons of water and simmer, covered, for 15 minutes, or until peas and fennel are just tender. Remove from the heat and let cool slightly.

Beat the eggs with the salt and black pepper in a bowl and fold in the cooked vegetables. Heat the butter in a large, heavy frying pan; when foaming, pour in the egg mixture. Cook over moderate heat until the bottom is nicely browned. Place under the broiler for 20 seconds to set the top. Follow directions for turning the *frittata* on page 202. Cook on the other side until the bottom is nicely browned. *Serves 3 or 4.*

*The Abruzzi*

## POTATO AND ONION FRITTATA
*(Frittata di patate)*

1    pound potatoes, peeled
¼    cup olive oil
1    large onion, thinly sliced
     Pinch of hot red pepper flakes
4    eggs
¼    teaspoon salt

Bring the potatoes to a boil in lightly salted boiling water and cook for 15 minutes, or until they are just tender. Drain, cool slightly, and cut into thin slices.

Heat half of the olive oil in a large frying pan and cook the onion and hot pepper over moderate heat for 3 minutes. Add the potatoes and cook for 5 minutes, or until they start to turn golden. Remove from the heat.

Beat the eggs with the salt and fold in the onion and potato mixture. Heat remaining olive oil in a large, heavy frying pan and pour in the egg mixture. Cook over moderate heat until the bottom is nicely browned. Place under the broiler for 20 seconds to set the top. Follow the directions for turning the *frittata* on page 202. Cook on the other side until the bottom is nicely browned. *Serves 3 or 4.*

*Veneto*

## MUSHROOM FRITTATA
*(Frittata con funghi)*

2   tablespoons olive oil
1   pound mushrooms, thinly sliced
2   tablespoons finely chopped fresh parsley
1   teaspoon flour
2   tablespoons dry Marsala wine
4   eggs
   Salt
   Freshly ground black pepper
2   tablespoons butter

Heat the olive oil in a frying pan and cook the mushrooms and parsley over moderate heat for 5 minutes. Add the flour and cook for 1 minute. Stir in the Marsala and cook for 1 more minute. Remove from heat and let cool.

Beat the eggs in a mixing bowl and season with ¼ teaspoon salt and a grinding of black pepper. Add the mushroom mixture and mix well. Heat the butter in a large, heavy frying pan; when foaming, pour in the egg mixture. Cook over moderate heat until the bottom is nicely browned. Place under the broiler for 20 seconds to set the top. Follow directions to turn the *frittata* on page 202. Cook on the other side until the bottom is nicely browned. *Serves 2 or 3.*

*Liguria*

## Swiss Chard Frittata
*(Frittata di bietole)*

The Swiss chard can be varied with any of the following green leafy vegetables: spinach, collards, turnip tops, watercress, or beet greens.

1   pound Swiss chard
2   tablespoons butter
1   garlic clove, crushed
2   teaspoons fresh marjoram, or ½ teaspoon dried
    Salt
    Freshly ground black pepper
⅛   teaspoon freshly grated nutmeg
½   cup freshly grated Parmesan cheese
5   eggs
½   cup whole-wheat bread crumbs, soaked in ¼ cup milk
2   tablespoons olive oil

Wash the Swiss chard and remove the ribs. Cook in a covered saucepan over moderate heat for 5 minutes. The water clinging to the leaves is sufficient to prevent scorching. Drain, and chop coarsely. Heat the butter in a small saucepan and cook the garlic and marjoram for 1 minute. Add the Swiss chard and simmer for 2 minutes. Season with salt, black pepper, and nutmeg. Remove from the heat and stir in the Parmesan cheese. Beat the eggs well and fold in the Swiss chard mixture and bread crumbs.

Heat the olive oil in a large frying pan and pour in the egg mixture. Cook over moderate heat until the bottom is nicely browned. Place under the broiler for 20 seconds to set the top. Follow the directions to turn the *frittata* on page 202. Cook on the other side until the bottom is nicely browned. *Serves 3 or 4.*

*Sicily*

## ARTICHOKE AND ASPARAGUS FRITTATA
### *(Millassata)*

2 artichokes
1/2 lemon
1/4 pound fresh asparagus
6 tablespoons olive oil
1 garlic clove, crushed
1 handful of fresh parsley, finely chopped
1/3 cup dry white wine
4 eggs
1/4 cup freshly grated Parmesan cheese
Salt
Freshly ground black pepper

Trim the artichokes and remove the leaves and chokes as described on page 226. Cut bottoms into slices 1/4 inch thick and rub with lemon to keep artichokes from discoloring. Trim the ends of the asparagus and peel the stalks with a sharp knife or vegetable peeler up to 2 inches from the tips. Steam for 15 minutes, or until they are tender.

Heat half of the olive oil in a frying pan and cook the garlic and parsley for 1 minute. Add the artichokes and cook over moderate heat for 5 minutes. Add the wine and cook until the wine has evaporated and the artichokes are lightly browned and tender.

Beat the eggs with the grated cheese. Fold in the cooked artichokes and asparagus. Season with salt and black pepper. Heat remaining 3 tablespoons oil in a large frying pan and pour in the egg mixture. Cook over moderate heat until the bottom is nicely browned. Place under the broiler for 20 seconds until the top is set. Follow directions for turning the frittata on page 202. Cook on the other side until the bottom is nicely browned. *Serves 3 or 4.*

*Campania*

## ONION AND CHEESE FRITTATA
### *(Frittata di cipolle e mozzarella)*

This may be served hot or cold and is perfect for a picnic.

¼   cup olive oil
2   large onions, thinly sliced
2   teaspoons chopped fresh basil, or ½
    teaspoon dried
4   eggs
¼   cup small dice of mozzarella cheese
    Salt
    Freshly ground black pepper

Heat 2 tablespoons of the olive oil in a frying pan and cook the onions and basil over moderate heat for 8 to 10 minutes, or until they are turning golden. Remove from heat and cool slightly.

Beat the eggs with the mozzarella cheese, and season with salt and black pepper. Stir in the onions. Heat remaining olive oil in a large, heavy frying pan and pour in the egg mixture. Cook over moderate heat until the bottom is nicely browned. Place under the broiler for 20 seconds until the top is set. Follow the directions for turning the frittata on page 202. Cook on the other side until the bottom is nicely browned. *Serves 3.*


*Sardinia*

## BAKED ZUCCHINI OMELET
### *(Frittata sardenaira)*

Baked omelets are made all over Italy. Easier to prepare than soufflés or *sformati*, they make a perfect dish for unexpected guests at lunch or supper.

  3  medium-size zucchini, about 1 pound
     altogether
¼  cup olive oil
  2  garlic cloves, crushed
  2  teaspoons fresh basil, or ½ teaspoon dried
  1  tablespoon finely chopped fresh parsley
  4  eggs
½  cup whole-wheat bread crumbs, soaked in
     ¼ cup milk
¼  cup freshly grated pecorino cheese
     Salt
     Freshly ground black pepper

Trim the ends of the zucchini and cut vegetables into thin slices. Heat the olive oil in a large frying pan and cook the garlic, basil, and parsley for 1 minute. Add the zucchini and cook over moderately high heat for 5 minutes, until the slices are tender and starting to turn golden. Remove from heat and cool slightly.

Beat the eggs well and stir in the bread crumbs and pecorino cheese. Season with salt and black pepper. Fold in the cooked zucchini and pour into a well-oiled shallow baking dish. Bake in a preheated 375°F. oven for 25 to 30 minutes, or until the top is golden and the center is set. Serve at once. *Serves 3 or 4.*

*Sardinia*

# BAKED PEA OMELET
### (Torta di piselli)

※ ※ ※

3   tablespoons olive oil
1   small onion, chopped
1   handful of parsley, finely chopped
2   cups shelled fresh peas
4   eggs
¼   cup freshly grated pecorino cheese
    Salt
    Freshly ground black pepper
½   cup fresh whole-wheat bread crumbs,
    soaked in ¼ cup milk

Heat the olive oil in a frying pan and cook the onion and parsley over moderate heat for 3 minutes. Add the peas and 2 to 3 tablespoons water and simmer, covered, for 15 minutes, or until the peas are tender. Beat the eggs in a mixing bowl with the grated cheese. Season with salt and black pepper. Stir in the bread crumbs and the onion and pea mixture. Pour into a well-oiled shallow baking dish. Bake in a preheated 375°F. oven for 25 to 30 minutes, or until the top is golden and the center is set. Serve at once. *Serves 3 or 4.*

*Tuscany*

# BAKED EGGPLANT OMELET
### *(Tortino di melanzane)*

This is a specialty of Florence. *Tortino* means
"pie" or "little pie" or "tartlet." This *tortino* is
very light and easy to prepare. For a variation,
try it with potatoes or zucchini.

1   **large eggplant, 1 to 1¹/₄ pounds**
    **Salt**
¹/₂  **cup olive oil**
5   **eggs**
¹/₃  **cup Tomato Sauce (page 57)**
¹/₂  **cup freshly grated Parmesan cheese**
    **Freshly ground black pepper**

Peel the eggplant and cut into slices ¹/₈ inch thick. Sprinkle with
salt and set in a colander for 1 hour to release the bitter juices.
Wash off the salt and pat slices dry. Fry slices in hot oil until they
are golden on both sides. Drain on paper towels.

Beat the eggs in a bowl and add the tomato sauce and Parmesan
cheese. Season with salt and black pepper.

Arrange the eggplant slices in the bottom of a well-oiled shallow
baking dish. Pour the egg mixture over the eggplant. Bake in a preheated 375°F. oven for 30 to 40 minutes, or until the top is golden
and the center is set. Serve at once. *Serves 4 or 5.*

*Tuscany*

## BAKED ARTICHOKE OMELET
*(Tortino di carciofi)*

Another Florentine specialty. This dish of deep-fried artichoke slices and beaten eggs is baked in the oven like a pie. It is well worth trying when artichokes are in season.

> 4   artichokes
> 1   lemon, cut in half
>     Flour
>     Oil for deep-frying
> 4   eggs
> 2   tablespoons milk
>     Salt
>     Freshly ground black pepper

Trim the artichokes and remove the leaves and chokes as described on page 226. Cut bottom into slices ¼ inch thick, and rub all over with lemon to keep them from discoloring. Dip slices into flour. Fry in hot oil until golden on both sides. Drain on paper towels. Beat the eggs in a bowl with the milk, and season with salt and black pepper. Arrange the fried artichokes in the bottom of a well-oiled shallow baking dish. Pour the egg mixture over them. Bake in a preheated 375°F. oven for 25 to 30 minutes, or until the top is golden and the eggs are set. *Serves 4.*

## Soufflés
*(Soffiati)*

A soufflé is basically a thick béchamel sauce mixed with egg yolks, a vegetable purée, and grated cheese or the flavoring of your choice. Stiffly beaten egg whites are folded in. The mixture is turned into a mold and baked in the oven until very puffed and browned.

To make a light soufflé, the egg whites must be beaten stiff, but do not overbeat so the egg whites become dry. Take care that the egg whites do not contain any particles of egg yolk or they will not rise stiffly. The best results are produced with a large wire whisk, but a hand beater or mixer is satisfactory.

The bowl used for egg whites must be absolutely free of moisture or grease. Unlined copper produces the best results as the acid in the copper helps to stabilize the egg whites, but stainless-steel or glass or porcelain make adequate substitutes.

Carefully fold one quarter of the egg whites into the warm sauce. Then *very lightly* fold in remaining egg whites. Turn into a well-buttered soufflé dish and place in the center of a preheated 400°F. oven. Turn the heat immediately down to 375°F. Bake for 30 to 35 minutes, until a knife comes out clean from the center of the soufflé. Serve immediately, as a cooked soufflé will start to sink rapidly after being removed from the oven.

*Lombardy*

## CHEESE SOUFFLÉ
### (Soffiato di formaggii)

   4  tablespoons butter
   5  tablespoons flour
1¹/₂  cups hot milk
 ¹/₂  cup grated Gruyère cheese
 ¹/₂  cup freshly grated Parmesan cheese
 ¹/₄  teaspoon freshly grated nutmeg
      Salt
      Freshly ground black pepper
   6  egg yolks

7   egg whites

Follow directions on page 61 and prepare a thick béchamel sauce with the butter, flour, and hot milk. Remove from the heat and stir in the Gruyère and Parmesan cheeses, the nutmeg, and salt and black pepper to taste. Add the egg yolks, one at a time, and mix well. Beat the egg whites stiff and fold one quarter of the whites into the sauce. Blend well. Lightly fold in remaining egg whites.

Pour into a well-buttered 8-cup soufflé dish. Place in a preheated 400°F. oven and reduce heat to 375°F. Bake for 30 to 35 minutes, or until the soufflé is well risen and the center is done. Serve at once. *Serves 6.*

*Emilia-Romagna*

## Eggplant Soufflé
### (Soffiato di melanzane)

1   medium-size eggplant, about ³/₄ pound
    Salt
    Flour
¹/₃  cup olive oil, approximately
4   tablespoons butter
5   tablespoons flour
1¹/₂ cups hot milk, or half milk and half broth
³/₄  cup freshly grated Parmesan cheese
    Freshly ground black pepper
6   egg yolks
7   egg whites

Peel the eggplant and cut into slices ¹/₄ inch thick. Sprinkle with salt and leave for 1 hour to release the bitter juices. Wash off the salt and pat dry. Dip the eggplant slices into flour and fry in hot oil

until golden on both sides. Force through a food mill or purée in
a blender. There should be approximately 1 to 1¼ cups purée.

Follow the directions on page 61 and prepare a thick béchamel
sauce with the butter, flour, and hot milk. Remove from heat and
stir in the Parmesan cheese, eggplant purée, and salt and black
pepper to taste. Add the egg yolks, one at a time, and mix well. Beat
the egg whites stiff and fold one quarter of the whites into the
sauce. Blend well. Lightly fold in remaining egg whites.

Pour into a well-buttered 8-cup soufflé dish. Place in the center of
a preheated 400°F. oven and reduce the heat to 375°F. Bake for
30 to 35 minutes or until the soufflé is well risen and the center is
done. Serve at once. *Serves 6.*

*Emilia-Romagna*

## SPINACH AND MUSHROOM SOUFFLÉ
*(Soffiato di spinaci e funghi)*

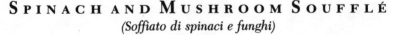

Soufflés can be made equally well with a sauce
made with broth instead of milk, which will
then be a velouté sauce. The result is deliciously savory and very light. Try it with this
flavorful combination of spinach and mushrooms.

    1   pound spinach
    2   tablespoons olive oil
    ½   pound mushrooms, thinly sliced
    4   tablespoons butter
    5   tablespoons flour
    1½  cups Vegetable Broth (page 69), hot

¹/₂  cup freshly grated Parmesan cheese
     Salt
     Freshly ground black pepper
¹/₄  teaspoon freshly grated nutmeg
 6   egg yolks
 7   egg whites

Wash the spinach and cook in a covered saucepan over moderate heat for 5 minutes. Drain, squeeze dry, and chop.

Heat the olive oil in a frying pan and cook the mushrooms over moderate heat for 5 minutes, or until they are tender and all the liquid has evaporated. Follow the directions on page 61 and prepare a thick velouté sauce with the butter, flour, and hot broth. Remove from the heat and stir in the Parmesan cheese, chopped spinach, mushrooms, salt and black pepper to taste, and the nutmeg.

Add the egg yolks, one at a time, and mix well. Beat the egg whites stiff and fold one quarter of the egg whites into the sauce. Blend well. Lightly fold in remaining egg whites.

Pour into a well-buttered 8-cup soufflé dish. Place in the center of a preheated 400°F. oven and reduce heat to 375°F. Bake for 30 to 35 minutes, or until the soufflé is well risen and the center is done. Serve at once. *Serves 6.*

## Molded Soufflés
### (Sformati)

*Sformati* are similar to regular soufflés except that they do not contain as many eggs. They are always cooked in a mold set in a pan of hot water. They do not rise as high as regular soufflés nor do they sink as quickly. *Sformati* are usually served unmolded on a serving platter.

*Tuscany*

## B R O C C O L I  M O L D E D  S O U F F L É
### *(Sformato di broccoli)*

This is very light and good.

2 cups broccoli flowerets
2 tablespoons olive oil
3 tablespoons butter
3 tablespoons flour
1 cup hot milk, or half milk and half broth
¼ cup freshly grated Parmesan cheese
    Salt
    Freshly ground black pepper
⅛ teaspoon freshly grated nutmeg
4 eggs, separated

Steam the broccoli flowerets for 7 minutes, or until they are just tender. Heat the olive oil in a frying pan and cook the broccoli over moderate heat for 3 minutes. Force through a food mill, or purée in a blender.

Follow the directions on page 61 and prepare a thick béchamel sauce with the butter, flour, and hot milk. Remove from the heat and stir in the Parmesan cheese, broccoli purée, salt and black pepper to taste, and the nutmeg.

Add the egg yolks, one at a time, and mix well. Beat the egg whites stiff and fold one quarter of the whites into the sauce. Blend well. Lightly fold in remaining egg whites.

Pour into a well-buttered 6-cup soufflé dish and set in a pan of hot water. Cook in the center of a preheated 350°F. oven for 30 minutes, or until a knife comes out clean from the center of the *sformato. Serves 4.*

*L a z i o*

## MOLDED PEA SOUFFLÉ
### *(Sformato di piselli)*

1   teaspoon olive oil
1   garlic clove, crushed
1   handful of fresh parsley, finely chopped
    Few leaves fresh mint, or a pinch of dried
    mint
2   cups shelled fresh peas
2   tablespoons butter
3   tablespoons flour
1   cup hot milk
¼   cup freshly grated Parmesan cheese
    Salt
    Freshly ground black pepper
4   eggs, separated

Heat the olive oil in a saucepan and cook the garlic, parsley, and mint for 1 minute. Add the peas and a little water and simmer, covered, for 15 minutes, or until the peas are tender and the liquid is evaporated. Force through a food mill or purée in a blender. Follow directions on page 61 and prepare a thick béchamel sauce with the butter, flour, and hot milk. Remove from heat and stir in the Parmesan cheese and salt and black pepper to taste.

Add the eggs, one at a time, and mix well. Beat the egg whites stiff and fold one quarter of the whites into the sauce. Blend well. Lightly fold in remaining egg whites.

Pour into a well-buttered 6-cup soufflé dish and set in a pan of hot water. Cook in the center of a preheated 350°F. oven for 30 minutes, or until a knife comes out clean from the center of the *sformato*. Serve at once. *Serves 6.*

# CHEESE

☙☙☙

## FORMAGGIO

Cheese is used frequently in Italian cooking, in soups, pasta, rice, polenta, and many vegetable dishes, but cheese cookery is limited. The most widely used cheeses for cooking are Parmesan, pecorino, mozzarella, and ricotta.

Parmesan cheese is probably the most famous of all Italian cheeses. Legally, cheese sold under this name is made in a carefully defined area around Parma and the neighboring cities of Reggio and Piacenza. However, good Parmesan cheese is made in many regions of Italy; it is sold under the name of Grana. Parmesan cheese is also excellent eaten as a sliced cheese. It comes in various qualities: Vecchio (old), which is two years old; Stravecchio (older), which is three years old; and the superior Stravecchione (extra old), which is at least four years old and can be aged for twenty years or even more. Parmesan cheese is extremely high in calcium; 100 grams (3½ ounces) has as much calcium as 1 quart of milk. It is also very high in protein. Weight for weight, sirloin steak has little more than two thirds of the amount of protein found in Parmesan cheese. Good Parmesan should be light yellow in color and sweat slightly. Always buy it whole and grate it just before using.

Pecorino, or pecorino romano as it is usually called in the United States, is another hard cheese similar to Parmesan that can be used for grating. It is made from ewe's milk and has a stronger flavor than Parmesan. Pecorino sardo or sardo is another type of pecorino that is made in Sardinia.

Asiago is a semi-fat hard cow's milk cheese that is also suitable for grating when it is aged over 12 months. It is made in the Province of Vicenza.

Mozzarella is a soft white cheese used throughout Italy. It originated in Naples where it is still made from buffalo's milk and eaten very fresh. Once this cheese has dried out it is only good for cooking. Elsewhere in Italy mozzarella is made from cow's milk. Fresh mozzarella is generally lightly wrapped and stored in water. It is obtainable at most Italian groceries.

Another cheese frequently used in Italian cooking is ricotta. It is a soft, fresh white cheese made from the whey of the milk. It is used as a filling for various pasta dishes and vegetable pies, in cheesecakes and some desserts. Fresh ricotta is easily obtainable at Italian markets. A commercial ricotta made from cow's milk can be found in most supermarkets. It is a good substitute and keeps considerably longer.

Caciocavallo is another cheese used for cooking in the South and Sicily. It is made from buffalo's or cow's milk and has a strong spicy flavor not unlike provolone.

Fontina cheese is used often in the cooking of Piedmont and the Valle d'Aosta where it is made. It is a soft, buttery cheese and is the basic ingredient of the famous Piedmontese dish *fonduta*.


*C a m p a n i a*

# Fried Mozzarella Sandwiches
### (*Mozzarella in carrozza*)

| | |
|---|---|
| 6 | slices of whole-wheat bread, cut into halves |
| 6 | ounces mozzarella |
| 2 | tablespoons milk |
| | Flour |
| 2 | eggs, beaten |
| 1/2 | cup olive oil |

Cut the mozzarella into thin slices and sandwich between the slices of bread. Sprinkle the sandwiches with milk and dip into flour. Let the sandwiches soak in the beaten eggs. Press the edges well together to enclose the cheese securely. Heat the olive oil in a frying pan and fry the sandwiches until golden on both sides. Serve at once. *Serves 6.*

*Campania*

## EGGPLANT AND MOZZARELLA TOASTS
### (Crostini di melanzane e mozzarella)

———— 🦋🦋🦋 ————

1 small eggplant, about ½ pound
  Salt
⅓ cup olive oil
4 slices of whole-wheat bread, toasted
½ cup Tomato Sauce (page 57)
4 slices of Gruyère cheese ⅛ inch thick, cut
  to the same size as the bread slices

Peel the eggplant and cut into slices ⅛ inch thick. Sprinkle with salt and set in a colander for 1 hour to release the bitter juices. Wash off the salt and pat slices dry with paper towels. Fry in hot oil until golden on both sides. Drain on paper towels. Arrange the fried eggplant over the slices of toast. Spread a little tomato sauce over the eggplant and top with slices of Gruyère cheese. Turn the broiler to high and broil until the cheese melts. Serve at once. *Serves 4.*

*L a z i o*

## CHEESE SKEWERS
### *(Spiedini di provatura)*

*Spiedini* are the Italian equivalent of the French *brochettes,* or skewers. They are morsels of food threaded on a skewer and grilled or deep-fried. The skewers are usually 6 inches long and made of wood, stainless steel, aluminum, or silver. Provatura cheese is a fresh buffalo's milk cheese made in the region of Rome. Mozzarella or fontina cheese make good substitutes.

| | |
|---|---|
| 6 | slices of whole-wheat bread, cut into quarters |
| 18 | slices of provatura cheese, cut to the same size as the bread quarters |
| 3 | or 4 plum tomatoes, cut into 18 slices ¼ inch thick |
| ⅓ | cup butter, melted |
| 6 | skewers |
| 18 | Italian or Greek black olives |

Thread the bread, cheese, and tomato slices on the skewers, beginning and ending with slices of bread. Cover the bottom of a baking dish with 3 tablespoons of melted butter. Arrange the skewers on top. Sprinkle with the remaining melted butter. Place under the broiler and toast the skewers until they are golden, turning them so they cook evenly. Serve at once, garnished with black olives. *Serves 6.*

*The North*

## CHEESE PUFFS
*(Bombole al formaggio)*

———— ❦ ❦ ❦ ————

These very light fritters are equally good with cocktails, as an antipasto or as a light lunch dish with a green salad on the side. They may be served with tomato sauce.

3  egg whites
   Salt
1  cup freshly grated Parmesan cheese
   Pinch of cayenne pepper
   Oil for deep-frying

Beat the egg whites with a little salt until stiff. Gradually fold in the grated cheese and the cayenne pepper. Drop by the teaspoon into hot oil and fry until golden on both sides. Do not overcrowd. Drain on paper towels and serve at once. *Serves 3.*

# VEGETABLES

## 🏵🏵🏵

## LEGUMI

Italians have been master market gardeners since Roman times. Many vegetables that are grown around the western world were first cultivated in Italy, which is why many of them are still called by Italian names—broccoli, zucchini, fava beans. Not only is the quality of vegetables in Italy unequalled in Europe, but because of the long growing season, vegetables are cheap and plentiful throughout the year.

Vegetables are always eaten fresh and in season. They are stuffed, sautéed, baked, broiled, stewed, gratinéed, or simply steamed and dressed with garlic, olive oil, and lemon juice. They appear in soufflés, *frittate* (omelets), puddings, tarts, with pasta or rice and they are, of course, the foundation of most Italian soups.

Herbs and spices of all kinds are used to enhance the natural flavor of the vegetables. Each region of Italy has its own special preferences. Marjoram is the favorite herb of Piedmont, mint is typical of Roman cooking, Calabria uses large amounts of ginger. Hot peppers *(peperoncini)* flavor many of the vegetable dishes of the South and Sicily.

### A R T I C H O K E S
### *(Carciofi)*

———— 🌿🌿🌿 ————

Several varieties of artichokes are grown in Italy. One is a long narrow, purplish variety that is so tender it can be eaten raw. Another is small and egg-shaped and is used for marinated artichokes. Then there is a large round variety called *mamme* or *mammola*, which is similar to the variety found in American supermarkets.

Italians love artichokes and cook them in many different ways. They may be boiled or steamed and served with a sauce on the side, or stuffed, deep-fried, stewed in wine and herbs, baked in a sauce, or served over pasta or risotto.

To steam or boil artichokes, cut off the top third of the leaves with a sharp knife or scissors and remove the stem. The heart or bottom will discolor quickly when cut, so rub at once with lemon juice. Never cook artichokes in an aluminum pan as it discolors them.

*Veneto*

## ARTICHOKES SIMMERED IN WINE
### (Carciofi alla Veneziana)

❦ ❦ ❦

6  globe artichokes
1  lemon, cut into halves
3  tablespoons olive oil
1  garlic clove, crushed
2  tablespoons fresh basil
1  cup dry white wine

Cut off the top 2 or 3 inches of the artichokes, removing all the tough, inedible dark green leaves. Trim the stem. Slice the artichokes lengthwise into halves and remove the fuzzy choke. Slice the remaining bottoms into slices ¼ inch thick. Rub all over with lemon to keep the artichokes from discoloring.

Heat the olive oil in a large frying pan and cook the garlic and basil for 1 minute. Add the artichokes and cook over moderate heat for 3 minutes. Add the wine, bring to a boil, cover, and simmer for 25 minutes, or until the artichokes are tender and the wine is reduced. *Serves 6.*

*Sicily*

## ARTICHOKES BRAISED WITH PEAS AND POTATOES
*(Carciofi con piselli e patate)*

This is a rich and flavorful combination. Do not overcook, so the vegetables retain their uniqueness.

   2   globe artichokes
   1/2  lemon
   3   tablespoons olive oil
   2   garlic cloves, crushed
   1   small onion, chopped
   2   tablespoons chopped parsley
   1   cup shelled fresh peas
   1/2  cup dry white wine
   1   pound tiny new potatoes, peeled
   1/2  cup boiling water
       Salt
       Freshly ground black pepper

Trim the artichokes and remove the leaves and chokes as described on page 226. Cut bottoms into slices 1/4 inch thick and rub all over with lemon to keep the artichokes from discoloring.

Heat the olive oil in a large frying pan and cook the garlic, onion, and parsley over moderate heat for 3 minutes. Add the artichoke slices and cook for 3 minutes longer. Add the peas and wine, bring to a boil, cover, and simmer for 10 minutes.

If the potatoes are tiny, leave them whole, otherwise cut into halves or quarters. Add to the artichokes and peas with the boiling water, and season with salt and black pepper. Cover and simmer for 25 to 30 minutes, or until the potatoes are tender and the liquid is evaporated. *Serves 6.*

*Tuscany*

# ARTICHOKES FLORENTINE
### *(Fondi di carciofi alla fiorentina)*

———— 🦪🦪🦪 ————

A delicious dish that may be served equally well as a vegetable accompaniment, a main course, or a buffet food. It can be prepared in advance and baked in the oven just before serving.

>  6   globe artichokes
>  2   pounds spinach
>  4   tablespoons butter
>     Salt
>     Freshly ground black pepper
>  1/8   teaspoon freshly grated nutmeg
>  2   cups Béchamel Sauce (page 61)
>  1/2   cup freshly grated Parmesan cheese
>  3   tablespoons bread crumbs

Trim the stems of the artichokes and steam for 45 minutes to 1 hour, or until the bottoms are tender and the outer leaves pull away easily. Set aside to cool. Wash the spinach carefully and cook in a covered saucepan with 2 tablespoons of the butter. The water clinging to the leaves will be sufficient to prevent scorching. Drain and chop coarsely. Season with nutmeg and salt and black pepper.

Remove all the outer leaves and the fuzzy chokes from the artichokes. Cut the bottoms into 1/4-inch-thick slices and arrange in a single layer in the bottom of a well-oiled shallow baking dish. Spread the cooked spinach over the top. Cover with a layer of hot béchamel sauce mixed with ¼ cup Parmesan cheese. Combine remaining Parmesan cheese with the bread crumbs and sprinkle over the top. Dot with remaining butter. Bake in a preheated 400°F. oven for 20 minutes, or until the top is golden. *Serves 6.*

*L o m b a r d y*

### ASPARAGUS, LOMBARD STYLE
*(Asparagii alla lombarda)*

Asparagus is usually eaten as an antipasto in Italy, with a simple dressing of olive oil and lemon juice, or with hot garlic-flavored oil and grated cheese. *Asparagii alla lombarda* is usually listed on Italian menus under the *Piatti del Giorno,* or "Today's Specials," and is served as a separate course. It may be served with fried or poached eggs.

1½  pounds asparagus
½   cup freshly grated Parmesan cheese
4   tablespoons butter, melted
4   poached eggs

Trim the ends of the asparagus and peel the stalks with a sharp knife or vegetable peeler up to about 2 inches from the tips. Steam for 15 minutes, or until they are tender.

Arrange asparagus on a serving platter and sprinkle with grated cheese. Dribble the melted butter over and top with poached eggs. Serve at once. *Serves 4.*

*Valle d'Aosta*

## BEETS IN CREAM
### *(Barbabietole alla crema)*

Save the beet tops for minestrone soup or a ravioli filling. They are too rich in vitamins and minerals to throw away.

1½  pounds beets
2  tablespoons olive oil
1  small onion, finely chopped
2  tablespoons chopped fresh parsley
1  teaspoon fresh marjoram or ¼ teaspoon dried
½  cup Vegetable Broth (page 69)
1  teaspoon lemon juice
¼  cup light cream

Bake the beets in a moderate oven for 45 minutes to 1½ hours, depending on their size. Slip off the skins and cut into slices ¼ inch thick. Heat the olive oil in a frying pan and cook the onion, parsley, and marjoram for 1 minute. Add the beets and cook over moderate heat for 2 minutes. Add the broth and lemon juice, bring to the boil, and simmer for 15 minutes until most of the liquid is evaporated. Stir in the cream and heat through. Serve at once. *Serves 4.*

*Emilia-Romagna*

## BEETS PARMIGIANA
### *(Barbabietole alla parmigiana)*

*Alla parmigiana* does not always mean that a dish comes from the city of Parma, but that the dish is sprinkled with Parmesan cheese. Sometimes vegetables *alla parmigiana* are baked in a white sauce topped with parmesan cheese, as in this recipe for beets parmigiana.

2 pounds beets, baked, with skins removed
3 cups Béchamel Sauce (page 61)
1 cup freshly grated Parmesan cheese
2 tablespoons butter

Cut the beets into thin slices and arrange a layer in a well-buttered shallow baking dish. Cover with a little béchamel sauce and sprinkle with a little grated cheese. Repeat the layers until all the ingredients are used. Top with Parmesan cheese and dot with butter. Bake in a preheated 375°F. oven for 20 to 25 minutes, or until the top is nicely browned. *Serves 6.*

*Tuscany*

## CRANBERRY BEANS IN RED WINE
*(Fagioli borlotti al vino rosso)*

Tuscany is famous for its bean dishes. The beans in this recipe are simmered in wine and cloves and enriched with a *soffritto* of olive oil, garlic, and rosemary. Towards the end of cooking the sauce is thickened with a little butter and flour.

2 cups dried cranberry beans
2 cups red wine
1 small onion, chopped
3 whole cloves
1/4 cup olive oil
1 quart water
3 garlic cloves, crushed
1 sprig of fresh rosemary, or 1/4 teaspoon dried
2 tablespoons butter
1 tablespoon whole-wheat flour
Salt
Freshly ground black pepper

Soak the beans in water overnight, and drain.

Place beans in a heavy saucepan with the red wine, onion, cloves, 2 tablespoons of the olive oil, and 1 quart water. Bring to a boil, cover, and simmer for 1 1/2 to 2 hours, or until the beans are tender. Meanwhile, heat remaining olive oil in a small frying pan and cook the garlic and rosemary for 1 minute. Add to the beans, stir well, and continue cooking. When the beans are tender, pour off and reserve the cooking liquid.

Heat the butter in a saucepan, stir in the flour, and cook over moderate heat for 1 minute. Slowly pour in the reserved bean cooking liquid. Season with salt and black pepper and simmer for 5 minutes. Add the drained beans, stir well, and simmer for 5 minutes more. *Serves 6.*

*Tuscany*

## WHITE BEANS WITH TOMATO AND SAGE
### *(Fagioli all'uccelletto)*

This is one of Tuscany's most famous bean dishes. *Fagioli all'uccelletto* literally means "beans like birds," supposedly because the sage, onion, garlic, and tomato flavoring makes the taste of the beans resemble small game birds.

  2  **cups dried white beans**
¼  **cup olive oil**
  2  **tablespoons butter**
  3  **garlic cloves, crushed**
10  **fresh sage leaves, or ½ teaspoon rubbed sage**
  1  **cup canned plum tomatoes, forced through a sieve or puréed in a food processor**
     **Salt**
     **Freshly ground black pepper**

Soak the beans in water overnight, and drain.

Place beans in a saucepan and cover with fresh water. Bring to a boil, cover, and simmer for 1½ to 2 hours, or until beans are tender. Drain.

Heat the olive oil and butter in a saucepan and cook the garlic and sage for 1 minute. Add the tomato purée and cook over moderate heat for 3 minutes. Add the drained beans and salt and black pepper to taste. Simmer for 5 more minutes. *Serves 6.*

*Sardinia*

## BEANS WITH FENNEL AND CABBAGE
### *(Fagioli alla gallurese)*

———— 🌿🌿🌿 ————

A simple peasant stew from the Northeast of Sardinia.

| | |
|---|---|
| 1½ | cups dried white beans |
| ¼ | cup olive oil |
| 2 | garlic cloves, crushed |
| 1 | onion, chopped |
| 3 | fennel bulbs |
| ½ | head of Savoy cabbage, shredded |
| 1 | cup canned plum tomatoes, forced through a sieve or puréed in a food processor |
| | Salt |
| | Freshly ground black pepper |

Soak the beans in water overnight, and drain.

Place beans in a saucepan and cover with fresh water. Bring to a boil, cover, and simmer for 1½ to 2 hours, or until beans are tender.

Meanwhile, heat the olive oil in a large saucepan and cook the garlic and onion over moderate heat for 5 minutes. Cut off the stems and coarse outer leaves of the fennel and cut the bulbs into thin strips. Add to the onion together with the shredded cabbage. Cover and simmer for 10 minutes, stirring occasionally. Add the tomato puree, cover, and simmer for 30 minutes, or until the fennel and cabbage are tender and the sauce is thickened.

When the beans are cooked, pour off and reserve 1 cup of the cooking liquid; discard the rest. Add the beans, 1 cup cooking liquid, and salt and black pepper to taste to the fennel and cabbage. Simmer together for 5 minutes. *Serves 4.*

*Piedmont*

## RATATOUILLE OF GREEN BEANS
### *(Fagiolini in umido)*

This is a specialty of Domodossola.

    2  pounds green beans
    2  tablespoons olive oil
    1  small onion, chopped
    2  garlic cloves, crushed
    2  tablespoons finely chopped fresh parsley
    1  teaspoon minced fresh basil, or ¼
       teaspoon dried
  ½  cup dry red wine
    1  cup canned plum tomatoes and their juice,
       seeded and chopped

Salt
Freshly ground black pepper

Trim the ends of the green beans and cut into 2-inch lengths. Heat the olive oil in a large frying pan and cook the onion, garlic, parsley, and basil for 1 minute. Add the red wine and cook over moderate heat until reduced by half. Add the tomatoes and cook gently for 15 minutes. Add the green beans, cover, and simmer for 15 minutes longer, or until the beans are tender and the sauce is thickened. *Serves 6.*

*Lazio*

## Turnip Tops with Garlic and Oil
### (Brocoletti con aglio e olio)

The Roman way of serving greens is simple and delicious. Swiss chard, beet greens, spinach, kale, collards and mustard greens can all be served the same way. If you like, the cooked greens can be dressed with a little extra olive oil, garlic, and a squeeze of lemon juice before serving.

3   tablespoons olive oil
3   cloves garlic, crushed
2   pounds turnip tops, cut into 3 inch lengths
    Salt
    Freshly ground black pepper

Heat the olive oil in a large saucepan and cook the garlic for 1 minute. Add the turnip tops and stir well. Cook, covered, over low heat for 8 to 10 minutes, or until the vegetables are tender, stirring occasionally so they cook evenly. Season with salt and black pepper to taste. *Serves 4.*

*Sicily*

## BROCCOLI BRAISED WITH LEEKS AND WHITE WINE
### *(Broccoli affogati)*

> 2 pounds broccoli
> 2 leeks
> 3 tablespoons olive oil
> 2 garlic cloves, crushed
> 1 handful of parsley, finely chopped
> ½ cup dry white wine
>   Salt
>   Freshly ground black pepper

Break the broccoli into flowerets and cut the stems into ½-inch dice. Steam for 7 to 8 minutes or until broccoli is almost tender. Do not overcook.

Meanwhile, trim away the roots of the leeks. Cut lengthwise into halves and carefully wash away any dirt that collects between the leaves. Cut into slices ½ inch thick.

Heat the olive oil in a large saucepan and cook the garlic and parsley for 1 minute. Add the leeks and dry white wine. Bring to the boil and simmer, covered, for 10 minutes or until leeks are tender, stirring from time to time so they cook evenly. Add the steamed broccoli and salt and black pepper to taste. Stir gently and simmer for 5 minutes. *Serves 6.*

*Emilia-Romagna*

# Brussels Sprouts Parmigiana
### *(Cavolini di bruxelles alla parmigiana)*

The Brussels sprouts are steamed and briefly cooked in butter, then dressed with Parmesan cheese, which gives them a delicious nutty flavor. Take care not to overcook them.

1½  **pounds Brussels sprouts**
2  **ounces butter**
¾  **cup freshly grated Parmesan cheese**
   **Salt**
   **Freshly ground black pepper**

Trim the root ends of the Brussels sprouts and remove any yellowish leaves. Steam for 8 to 10 minutes, or until they are just tender. Heat the butter in a large frying pan. Add the sprouts and stir well to coat them evenly with butter. Sprinkle with Parmesan cheese and salt and black pepper to taste. Stir again and serve at once. *Serves 6.*

*All Italy*

# SWEET-AND-SOUR CABBAGE WITH CAPERS
### (Cavolo in agrodolce)

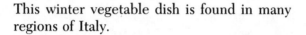

This winter vegetable dish is found in many regions of Italy.

2 tablespoons olive oil
1 small onion, chopped
1 head of green cabbage, shredded
2 tablespoons hot water
1 cup canned plum tomatoes, forced through a sieve or puréed in a food processor
2 tablespoons wine vinegar
1 tablespoon capers
2 teaspoons sugar or honey
 Salt
 Freshly ground black pepper

Heat the olive oil in a large saucepan and cook the onion over moderate heat for 3 minutes. Add the shredded cabbage and hot water, and simmer, covered, for 10 minutes, stirring occasionally so the cabbage cooks evenly. Add the tomato purée, vinegar, capers, sugar, and salt and black pepper to taste; stir well. Cover and simmer for 30 minutes, or until the cabbage is very tender and the sauce is reduced. *Serves 6.*

*Liguria*

## CARROT FRICASSEE
*(Carote in fricassèa)*

|       |                                  |
|-------|----------------------------------|
| 3     | tablespoons butter               |
| 2     | tablespoons finely chopped parsley |
| 1½    | pounds carrots, diced            |
| 3     | tablespoons hot water            |
| 2     | egg yolks                        |
| ½     | cup heavy cream                  |
|       | Salt                             |
|       | Freshly ground black pepper      |

Heat the butter in a saucepan and cook the parsley and carrots for 3 minutes. Add 3 tablespoons hot water, cover, and simmer for 20 minutes, or until carrots are tender and the liquid is evaporated. Beat the egg yolks and cream together and pour over the carrots. Cook over moderate heat until the sauce is slightly thickened. Do not boil. Season with salt and black pepper to taste. Serve at once. *Serves 6.*

*Tuscany*

## CAULIFLOWER AND POTATO PIE
*(Pasticcio do cavolfiore e patate)*

|       |                                     |
|-------|-------------------------------------|
| 1     | small cauliflower, about 1½ pounds  |
| 1½    | pounds potatoes, peeled             |
| 3     | ounces butter                       |
| ¼     | cup heavy cream                     |
| ⅛     | teaspoon freshly grated nutmeg      |

Salt
Freshly ground black pepper
3 tablespoons bread crumbs or wheat germ

Cut the cauliflower into sections and steam for 10 minutes or until it is tender. Bring the potatoes to boil in lightly salted water and cook for 20 minutes, or until they are tender. Force the cauliflower and potatoes through a food mill or sieve. Add half of the butter, the cream, nutmeg, and salt and black pepper to taste; mix well.

Oil a baking dish and sprinkle with bread crumbs. Turn the dish over and shake out any excess crumbs. Spoon in the cauliflower and potato mixture. Melt remaining butter in a small pan and dribble over the top. Bake in a preheated 350°F. oven for 30 minutes, or until the top is golden. *Serves 6.*

*L o m b a r d y*

## CELERY GRATIN
*(Sedani gratinati)*

————— 𝕂𝕂𝕂 —————

This is a specialty of Verona.

2 bunches of celery
2 tablespoons olive oil
3 cups Béchamel Sauce (page 61)
½ cup grated Gruyère cheese
⅛ teaspoon freshly grated nutmeg
Salt
Freshly ground black pepper
2 tablespoons freshly grated Parmesan cheese
2 tablespoons bread crumbs or wheat germ

  2  tablespoons butter

Remove the root ends and the leaves of the celery. Cut ribs into 2-inch lengths and steam for 10 minutes, or until they are tender. Heat the olive oil in a large frying pan and cook the celery over moderate heat until it is golden on both sides.

Prepare a béchamel sauce. Remove from the heat and stir in the Gruyère cheese, nutmeg, and salt and black pepper to taste. Spoon some of the sauce into the bottom of a large shallow baking dish. Arrange the celery on top. Pour the remaining sauce over the celery. Combine the Parmesan cheese with the bread crumbs and sprinkle over the top. Dot with butter. Bake in a preheated 400°F. oven for 20 minutes, or until the top is golden. *Serves 4.*

*Liguria*

## EGGPLANT AND TOMATO GRATIN
### *(Melanzane e pomodoro gratinati)*

This is one of my favorite baked vegetable dishes; it has a wonderful Mediterranean flavor.

2 or 3    medium-size eggplants, about 2 pounds altogether
           Salt
  ³/₄    cup olive oil, approximately
   2    garlic cloves, crushed
   1    handful of parsley, chopped
   2    pounds ripe plum tomatoes, peeled, seeded, and chopped
           Freshly ground black pepper

1  cup whole-wheat bread crumbs
2  tablespoons freshly grated Parmesan
   cheese

Peel the eggplant and cut into slices ⅛ inch thick. Sprinkle with salt and set in a colander for 1 hour to release the bitter juices. Wash off the salt and pat slices dry. Fry slices in hot oil until golden on both sides. Drain on paper towels.

Heat 2 tablespoons of olive oil in a large frying pan and cook the garlic and parsley for 1 minute. Add the tomatoes and cook over moderate heat for 15 minutes. Season with salt and black pepper.

Place a layer of eggplant on the bottom of a shallow baking dish. Spread a little of the tomato mixture over the top and sprinkle lightly with bread crumbs. Repeat layers until all the ingredients are used, ending with bread crumbs. Sprinkle the top with Parmesan cheese and dribble 2 tablespoons olive oil over the top. Bake in a preheated 350°F. oven for 30 to 35 minutes, or until the top is golden. *Serves 4 to 6.*

*Campania and the South*

# BROILED EGGPLANT SLICES
### *(Melanzane alla griglia)*

2  medium-size eggplants, about 1¼ pounds
   altogether
½  cup olive oil, approximately
1½  cups Tomato Sauce (page 57)
1½  cups freshly grated Parmesan cheese

Trim the ends of the eggplants, but do not peel. Cut into slices ½ inch thick. Arrange slices in a single layer on a well-oiled baking sheet, and brush each slice liberally with olive oil. Cover with aluminum foil. Bake in a preheated 400°F. for 15 minutes, or until the eggplant is tender but not mushy.

Remove the foil. Spread a little tomato sauce over each eggplant slice and sprinkle with Parmesan cheese. Set the broiler to high and broil for a few minutes, until the tops are golden. *Serves 4 to 6.*

*Liguria*

# FUNGHETTO
## (Funghetto)

※※※

This is a simple dish of fried eggplant, zucchini, and mushrooms. *Funghetto* means "cooked like mushrooms"—or cooked in olive oil, garlic, and herbs.

- ½ cup olive oil
- 2 garlic cloves, crushed
- 1 handful of parsley, finely chopped
- 1 tablespoon fresh oregano, or ½ teaspoon dried
- 2 small eggplants, unpeeled and cut into ½-inch cubes
- 2 small zucchini, sliced
- ¼ pound mushrooms, sliced
  Salt
  Freshly ground black pepper

Heat the olive oil in a large frying pan and cook the garlic, parsley, and oregano for 1 minute. Add the eggplant cubes, zucchini slices, and mushrooms and cook, covered, over moderate heat for 10 minutes, or until the vegetables are tender and turning golden. Season with salt and black pepper. Simmer for another 2 minutes. *Serves 6.*

*C a m p a n i a*

## EGGPLANT SAUTÉED WITH TOMATOES AND HERBS
*(Melanzane al funghetto)*

Fresh plum tomatoes are best for this recipe. If they are unavailable, canned plum tomatoes may be used, but take care to drain off any juice before adding them to the eggplant.

  2  medium-size eggplants, about 1¹/₄ pounds altogether
 ³/₄ cup olive oil, approximately
  2  garlic cloves, crushed
  1  tablespoon fresh basil, or ¹/₄ teaspoon dried
  1  tablespoon chopped fresh parsley
  1  tablespoon fresh oregano, or ¹/₄ teaspoon dried
  6  ripe plum tomatoes, peeled, seeded, and cut into strips
     Salt
     Freshly ground black pepper

Trim the ends of the eggplant and do not peel. Cut into ¹/₂-inch cubes. Heat the oil in a large frying pan and cook the garlic, basil, parsley, and oregano for 1 minute. Add the eggplant cubes, cover, and simmer for 30 minutes, stirring occasionally, until the eggplant is tender. Add the tomatoes and salt and black pepper to taste. Cover, and simmer for 10 minutes more. *Serves 4.*

*Emilia-Romagna and the North*

# FENNEL GRATIN
### *(Finocchii gratinati)*

6    fennel bulbs
2    cups Béchamel Sauce (page 61)
2    tablespoons freshly grated Parmesan cheese
¼    cup whole-wheat bread crumbs, or wheat germ
2    tablespoons butter

Remove the stems and coarse outer leaves from the fennel bulbs. Trim the bases and cut into quarters. Steam the pieces for 30 to 40 minutes, until they are just tender.

Prepare the béchamel sauce and spoon a little in the bottom of a shallow baking dish. Arrange the fennel on top in a single layer. Pour remaining sauce over the vegetable. Combine the Parmesan cheese and the bread crumbs and sprinkle over the top. Dot with butter. Bake in a preheated 400°F. oven for 20 minutes, or until the top is golden. *Serves 6.*

*Apulia*

# LEEKS BRAISED WITH CARROTS AND TOMATOES
### *(Porri in stufato)*

This is a light and delicious combination.

6  leeks
3  tablespoons olive oil
2  small carrots, diced
6  ripe plum tomatoes, peeled, seeded, and
   chopped
   Salt
   Freshly ground black pepper

Trim away the root ends of the leeks. Cut leeks lengthwise into
halves and carefully wash away any dirt that collects between the
leaves. Cut into 2-inch lengths. Use the whole leek, including the
dark green parts. Heat the olive oil in a large saucepan and cook
the leeks and carrots, covered, over moderate heat for 5 minutes.
Add the tomatoes, cover, and simmer for 30 minutes. Season with
salt and black pepper and serve at once. *Serves 4 to 6.*

*Lombardy*

# LENTIL PURÉE WITH CREAM
### *(Purè di lenticchie)*

2  cups green lentils
1  bay leaf

2 tablespoons olive oil
1 garlic clove, crushed
1 onion, finely chopped
1 celery rib, thinly sliced
2 tablespoons finely chopped fresh parsley
Pinch of ground cloves
Salt
Freshly ground black pepper
2 tablespoons butter
¹/₄ cup heavy cream

Soak the lentils in water overnight and drain. Place in a saucepan with the bay leaf, cover with fresh water, and bring to a boil. Cover and simmer for 1¹/₂ hours, or until the lentils are soft. Remove the bay leaf. Heat the olive oil in another saucepan and cook the garlic, onion, celery, and parsley over moderate heat for 5 minutes. Add to the lentils, together with the cloves and salt and black pepper to taste. If necessary, increase the heat slightly to reduce the cooking liquid. Cook for 15 minutes more.

Force lentils through a food mill or purée in a blender. Return to the pan. Stir in the butter and the cream, and simmer for 5 more minutes. Serve at once. *Serves 6.*

*Liguria*

## MUSHROOMS WITH PINE NUTS
*(Funghi trifolati con pignoli)*

2 tablespoons olive oil
1 garlic clove, crushed
1 small onion, finely chopped
1 tablespoon chopped fresh parsley

1 tablespoon fresh marjoram, or ¼ teaspoon
   dried
1½ pounds mushrooms, sliced
½ cup pine nuts
   Salt
   Freshly ground black pepper

Heat the olive oil in a frying pan and cook the garlic, onion, parsley, and marjoram over moderate heat for 3 minutes. Add the mushrooms and pine nuts, and stir well. Cook over moderate heat for 5 minutes, or until the mushrooms are tender. *Serves 4 to 6.*

*Piedmont*

## BRAISED ONIONS AND PEAS
*(Cipolle e piselli in umido)*

2 tablespoons olive oil
1 garlic clove, crushed
2 tablespoons finely chopped fresh parsley
1 pound small white onions, peeled
2 cups shelled fresh peas
½ cup Vegetable Broth (page 69), hot
   Salt
   Freshly ground black pepper
2 tablespoons heavy cream

Heat the olive oil in a saucepan and cook the garlic and parsley for 1 minute. Add the onions, peas, and broth. Cover and simmer for 20 to 25 minutes, or until the peas are tender and the liquid is evaporated. Season with salt and black pepper to taste. Stir in the cream. Heat through and serve at once. *Serves 6.*

*Valle d'Aosta*

## SPLIT-PEA CREAM
*(Purè di piselli)*

1    cup split peas
2    tablespoons olive oil
1    leek, thinly sliced
¼    head of Boston lettuce, shredded
4    cups Vegetable Broth (page 69) or water
3    tablespoons butter
     Salt
     Freshly ground black pepper

Soak the split peas in water overnight, and drain.

Heat the olive oil in a saucepan and cook the leek over moderate heat for 5 minutes, stirring from time to time so the leek cooks evenly. Add the lettuce, split peas, and broth. Bring to a boil, cover, and simmer for 1¼ to 1½ hours, or until the split peas are tender. Force through a food mill or purée in a blender. Return purée to the pan and add the butter and salt and black pepper to taste. Simmer for 5 minutes. *Serves 4.*

*The Abruzzi*

## GOLDEN FRIED SWEET PEPPERS
### *(Peperoni dorati)*

Italians love deep-fried vegetables. This dish is very simple to prepare. The sweet peppers are cut into strips, dipped into flour, then into beaten egg, and deep-fried until crisp and golden. Sometimes a little grated Parmesan cheese is added to enhance the flavor. Zucchini, eggplant, mushrooms, and onions all make suitable variations.

6  green sweet peppers
   Whole-wheat flour
2  eggs, beaten
   Oil for deep-frying
6  lemon wedges

Broil the sweet peppers until they are blackened all over. Wash under cold water and remove the skins. Cut into strips about 1 inch wide. Dip into flour, then into beaten egg. Fry in hot oil until golden on both sides. Drain on paper towels. Serve at once, with lemon wedges on the side. *Serves 6.*

*Liguria*

## POTATOES WITH WALNUTS
### *(Patate alla provinciale)*

This is deliciously exotic and full of flavor.

 2  pounds waxy potatoes
 2  tablespoons olive oil
 2  tablespoons butter
 2  garlic cloves, crushed
 1  teaspoon fresh basil, or ¼ teaspoon dried
 1  handful of parsley, chopped
 1  small onion, finely chopped
    Grated rind of 1 lemon
    Salt
    Freshly ground black pepper
    Juice of ½ lemon
 ¼  cup shelled walnuts, ground in the blender

Peel the potatoes and cut into slices ⅛ inch thick. Heat the olive oil and butter in a large frying pan and cook the garlic, basil, parsley, onion, and lemon rind over moderate heat for 5 minutes. Add the sliced potatoes, and sprinkle with salt and black pepper. Continue to cook until the potatoes are golden on both sides. Sprinkle with lemon juice and ground walnuts. Toss lightly and serve at once. *Serves 4 to 6.*

*Campania*

## POTATOES WITH TOMATOES
### *(Patate alla pizzaiola)*

1½   pounds waxy potatoes, peeled
2    garlic cloves, crushed
3    tablespoons olive oil
6    ripe plum tomatoes, peeled, seeded and
     chopped
1    tablespoon fresh basil, or ½ teaspoon dried
     Salt
     Freshly ground black pepper

Bring the potatoes to boil in lightly salted water and cook for 20 minutes, or until the potatoes are tender. Drain, and cut into slices. Heat the olive oil in a large frying pan and cook the garlic for 1 minute. Add the chopped tomatoes and cook over moderate heat for 8 minutes. Add the potatoes and basil, and season with salt and black pepper to taste. Simmer for 5 more minutes to blend the flavors. *Serves 4 to 6.*

*Veneto*

## ZUCCHINI, VENETIAN STYLE
### *(Zucchini alla veneta)*

2    pounds zucchini
2    tablespoons butter
3    tablespoons olive oil
2    tablespoons finely chopped parsley

2  whole eggs plus 1 egg yolk
¼  cup freshly grated Parmesan cheese
   Salt
   Freshly ground black pepper

Trim the ends of the zucchini and cut into rounds ⅛ inch thick. Heat the butter and olive oil in a large frying pan and cook the zucchini and parsley over moderately high heat until slices are golden on both sides. Beat the whole eggs, egg yolk, Parmesan cheese, and salt and black pepper to taste together, and pour over the zucchini. Stirring constantly, cook for 1 or 2 minutes, or until the zucchini are evenly coated. Serve at once. *Serves 6.*

# DESSERTS

### DOLCI

Italians usually end their meals with fresh fruit with or without some cheese.

Cakes and pastries are usually bought in pastry shops, or eaten in the middle of the afternoon with a cup of coffee.

In this chapter I have a selection of cakes and fruit desserts that can be quickly and easily made in American kitchens, and a few traditional custards and creams that are suited to family meals and informal entertaining.

Many of the recipes I have chosen are traditionally sweetened with honey. In most cases either honey or sugar may be used according to your preference.

*Veneto*

## PUMPKIN CAKE
### *(Torta di zucca)*

This is a moist cake with a delicious flavor.

1   cup unbleached white flour

1   cup whole-wheat pastry flour
2¹/₂   teaspoons baking soda
2   teaspoons baking powder
¹/₄   teaspoon salt
1   teaspoon ground cinnamon
¹/₄   teaspoon freshly grated nutmeg
2   cups purée of cooked pumpkin
³/₄   cup bland oil (soy or peanut oil is best)
1   cup honey
2   tablespoons rum
3   eggs
    Grated rind of 1 lemon
1   cup light raisins

Butter and flour a tube pan 10 × 4 inches. Combine the flours, baking soda, baking powder, salt, cinnamon, and nutmeg in a bowl and set aside. Beat the pumpkin purée with the oil in a large mixing bowl. Gradually stir in the honey and the rum. Beat the eggs well and add, one third at a time, to the mixture, blending well after each addition. Fold in the dry ingredients, blending well. Lastly, stir in the grated lemon rind and the raisins. Turn into the prepared pan. Bake in the lower third of a preheated 350°F. oven for 50 to 60 minutes, or until a cake tester comes out clean from the center of the cake. Let the cake cool in the pan for 10 minutes, then gently invert onto a cake rack to cool completely. *Serves 12 to 16.*

*Tuscany*

## ALMOND SPONGE CAKE
### *(Bocca di dama)*

—— 🦋🦋🦋 ——

*Bocca di dama* literally means "Milady's mouth," probably to point out that this cake is fine enough for an aristocrat.

6 large eggs, separated
½ cup sugar
⅓ cup unblanched almonds, finely ground in a blender
1 cup whole wheat flour
Grated rind of 1 lemon

Butter a 9-inch springform pan and dust with flour. Beat the egg yolks with the sugar until very light. Add the ground almonds, flour, and lemon rind and blend well together. Beat the egg whites stiff and carefully fold into the mixture. Pour into the prepared pan. Bake in a preheated 325°F. oven for 40 minutes or until a cake tester comes out clean from the center of the cake. *Serves 6 to 8.*

*Liguria*

# CORNMEAL APPLE CAKE
## (Torta di mele)

This is a simple rustic dessert. Use the coarse cornmeal found in Italian groceries.

½   cup whole-wheat flour
½   cup cornmeal
2   teaspoons baking powder
½   teaspoon salt
¼   teaspoon freshly grated nutmeg
¼   teaspoon grated mace
5   or 6 apples
2   tablespoons lemon juice
½   teaspoon ground cinnamon
2   eggs
¾   cup milk
½   cup sugar
⅓   cup melted butter

Butter a 9-inch springform pan and dust with flour. Combine the flour, cornmeal, baking powder, salt, nutmeg, and mace in a large bowl and set aside. Peel, quarter, and slice the apples, and sprinkle them with lemon juice and cinnamon. Beat the eggs lightly and add the milk, sugar, and melted butter. Stir liquids into the flour mixture. The batter will be thin. Fold in the apples and pour into the prepared pan. Bake in a preheated 350°F. oven for 35 to 40 minutes, or until the top is golden. *Serves 6.*

*Emilia-Romagna*

## CARROT ALMOND TORTE
*(Torta di carote)*

Flour
2 cups finely grated carrots
2 cups shelled almonds, finely ground in a
blender
1/2 cup bread crumbs
2 teaspoons baking powder
4 eggs, separated
1/2 cup sugar
1 tablespoon brandy
Grated rind of 1 lemon

Butter a 9-inch springform pan and dust with flour. Combine the carrots, ground almonds, bread crumbs, and baking powder in a large bowl and set aside. Beat the egg yolks and sugar until light and add to the carrot mixture, blending well. Stir in the brandy and the lemon rind. Beat the egg whites stiff and fold into the mixture. Pour into the prepared pan. Bake in a preheated 325°F. oven for 50 to 60 minutes or until a cake tester comes out clean from the center of the cake. *Serves 6 to 8.*

*Lazio*

# ROMAN CHEESECAKE
### *(Torta di ricotta)*

Italian cheesecakes are less rich than American cheesecakes, and very simple to prepare. Candied fruits are usually included in this recipe, but I prefer to use dried apricots instead.

    Flour
3   cups ricotta cheese
3   tablespoons unbleached white flour
⅓   cup sugar or honey
3   eggs, separated
¼   cup light raisins
2   tablespoons dried apricots, diced very small
3   tablespoons rum or sweet Marsala wine
½   teaspoon vanilla extract
    Grated rind of 1 lemon

Butter an 8-inch springform pan and dust with flour.

Combine the ricotta cheese, flour, honey, and egg yolks in a large bowl and beat until very smooth. Stir in the raisins, dried apricots, rum, vanilla extract, and lemon rind. Beat the egg whites stiff and fold into the mixture. Pour into the prepared pan. Bake in a preheated 350°F. oven for 40 to 45 minutes, or until the top is golden and a cake tester comes out clean from the center of the cake. *Serves 6.*

*Alto Adige*

## APPLE STRUDEL
*(Apfelstrudel)*

The Austrian influence is still very strong in the Alto Adige, and this is reflected in many of the delicious pastries and strudels that are made in the region. It is easy to make perfect apple strudel with commercial strudel dough or filo pastry. Be sure to allow at least 2 hours for the pastry to thaw out and be ready for use. If you wish to make the pastry yourself follow the directions for the pastry on page 154.

  5   sheets of filo pastry, 12 × 16 inches, thawed
  ⅓   cup olive oil, approximately
  4   large apples
  ⅓   cup raisins
  ¼   cup shelled almonds, finely ground in the blender
  2   tablespoons pine nuts
  ¼   cup wheat germ
      Grated rind of 1 lemon
  1   teaspoon ground cinnamon
  ¼   cup honey or sugar
  2   tablespoons butter, melted

Cover the table or countertop with a clean cloth. Lay a sheet of filo pastry on the cloth and brush lightly with oil. Place another sheet of pastry on top and repeat until all 5 sheets have been brushed with oil. Peel, core, and slice the apples thinly and arrange over one third of the pastry nearest to you. Sprinkle with raisins, ground almonds, pine nuts, wheat germ, and lemon rind. Sprinkle with cinnamon and dribble the honey and then the melted butter over the top. Carefully pick up the corners of the cloth closest to you and gently lift the cloth and let the strudel roll over once. Brush the top lightly with oil and then lift the cloth again and let the strudel roll over completely. Brush the top lightly with oil. Pick up the cloth, together with the strudel, and very carefully twist onto a greased baking sheet. Brush the top with oil. Bake in the lower third of a preheated 350°F. oven for 35 to 40 minutes, or until the apples are just tender and the pastry is crisp and golden. Let cool before serving. *Serves 6.*

*L o m b a r d y*

## APPLE CHARLOTTE FLAMBÉ
### *(Ciarlotta di mele)*

- 2   pounds apples
- ¼   pound butter, melted
- 3   tablespoons honey or sugar
- ½   cup light raisins
- ¼   cup pine nuts
-     Grated rind of 1 lemon
- 7   or 8 slices of bread
- ¾   cup rum, approximately

Peel, core, and slice the apples. Heat 2 tablespoons butter and add the apples and honey. Simmer until the mixture has the consistency of a thick purée. Remove from heat and add the raisins, pine nuts, and lemon rind. Butter a charlotte mold or a deep cake tin. Dip the bread into the melted butter and line the bottom and sides of the mold tightly with bread slices. Fill with the apple mixture. Top with remaining slices of bread and brush the top with melted butter. Bake in a preheated 350°F. oven for 35 to 40 minutes, or until the top is golden. Carefully turn out onto a serving dish. Pour the rum over the charlotte and ignite the rum.

Keep the apple filling thick. If it is too liquid it would soften the
bread too much and the charlotte would collapse when turned out
of the mold. *Serves 6.*

*Alto Adige*

## PEAR AND ALMOND PUDDING
*(Torta di pere e mandorle)*

❦ ❦ ❦

This simple dessert is a favorite with children.
Apples make a delicious variation.

3/4  cup whole-wheat bread crumbs
6  Anjou pears
1/4  cup shelled almonds, finely ground in a
    blender
1/3  cup raisins
1/4  cup sugar
    Grated rind of 1 lemon
3  tablespoons butter
1/2  cup water

Butter a baking dish and sprinkle the bottom and sides with bread
crumbs. Peel, core, and slice the pears and place a layer over the
bottom of the baking dish. Sprinkle with ground almonds, raisins,
sugar, and grated lemon rind. Sprinkle with more bread crumbs
and dot with butter. Repeat the layers until all the ingredients are
used, ending with bread crumbs and butter. Pour in 1/2 cup water.
Bake in a preheated 350°F. oven for 30 to 40 minutes, or until the
pears are tender and the top is golden. *Serves 4 to 6.*

*Veneto*

## CORNMEAL COOKIES WITH RAISINS AND PINE NUTS
### *(Zaletti)*

———— 🌿🌿🌿 ————

*Zaletti* are traditional Venetian raisin cookies, made with a mixture of cornmeal and wheat flour, flavored with lemon rind, vanilla, and pine nuts. *Zaletti* means "yellow."

| | |
|---|---|
| ½ | cup raisins |
| ¼ | cup brandy |
| 1½ | cups whole-wheat flour |
| 1 | cup cornmeal |
| ¼ | teaspoon salt |
| 3 | egg yolks |
| ½ | cup honey |
| ½ | cup melted butter |
| ⅓ | cup pine nuts |
| | Grated rind of 1 lemon |
| ½ | teaspoon vanilla extract |

Place the raisins in a small bowl and pour the brandy over them. Let them steep for 1 to 2 hours.

Combine the flour, cornmeal, and salt in a large bowl and set aside. Beat the egg yolks with the honey until light. Add to the flour and cornmeal mixture, together with the melted butter, the raisins soaked in brandy, the pine nuts, lemon rind, and vanilla. Mix to a soft dough. Roll out to ⅛ inch thick and cut into diamond shapes. Arrange cookies on a well-buttered cookie sheet. Bake in a preheated 375°F. oven for 10 to 15 minutes, or until the cookies are turning golden. *Makes about 36 cookies.*

*Lombardy*

## APPLE FRITTERS
### *(Laciaditt)*

|   |   |
|---|---|
| 2 | cups whole-wheat or unbleached white flour |
| 1/2 | teaspoon salt |
| 2 | eggs, separated |
| 1/3 | cup rum |
| 1 | cup water |
| 4 | or 5 apples |
|   | Oil for deep-frying |
|   | Sugar or honey |
| 1 | lemon |

Combine the flour and salt in a bowl and make a well in the center. Add the egg yolks, 1 tablespoon of rum, and half of the water. Blend well together. Gradually stir in remaining water until the batter is smooth. Let stand for 1 hour.

Peel and core the apples and cut into rounds 1/8 inch thick. Place in a shallow bowl and pour remaining rum over them. Let the apples steep for 30 minutes.

Beat the egg whites stiff and fold into the batter. Dip the apple rings into the batter and fry in hot oil until golden on both sides. Drain on paper towels, dust with sugar, and serve at once, with lemon wedges on the sides. *Serves 4 to 6.*

*Sicily*

## ORANGES AND CURAÇAO
### *(Arance e Curaçao)*

Light and refreshing.

6 large oranges
¾ cup Curaçao liqueur
2 tablespoons honey, warmed

Peel the oranges and remove all the white pith. Cut into slices ⅛ inch thick, and pick out any seeds. Place slices in a glass serving dish. Mix the Curaçao with the warmed honey until honey is dissolved. Pour the liqueur over the orange slices. Chill thoroughly before serving. *Serves 6.*

*Lazio*

## STRAWBERRIES WITH ORANGE JUICE
### *(Fragole al arancia)*

1 quart strawberries
Juice of 2 oranges
2 tablespoons honey, warmed
1 tablespoon Curaçao liqueur

Wash and hull the strawberries and place in individual glass dishes. Stir the warmed honey into the orange juice until the honey is dissolved. Add the Curaçao liqueur and pour over the strawberries. Chill thoroughly before serving. *Serves 4.*

*Piedmont*

# STRAWBERRIES WITH RICOTTA CREAM
## *(Ricotta con le fragole)*

Ricotta cheese is used extensively in Italian desserts. In this recipe the ricotta is mixed with egg yolks, milk, cream, and a dash of liqueur. This makes a delicious alternative to whipped cream.

| | |
|---|---|
| 1 | quart strawberries |
| 2 | cups ricotta cheese |
| 2 | egg yolks |
| 2 | tablespoons rum |
| | Grated rind of 1 lemon |
| 1/4 | cup honey or sugar |
| 1/4 | cup heavy cream, whipped |

Wash and hull the strawberries and place in individual glass dishes. Force the ricotta cheese through a fine sieve into a mixing bowl. Add the egg yolks, rum, lemon rind, and honey, and blend well together. Fold in the whipped cream. Spoon the mixture over the strawberries. Chill thoroughly before serving. *Serves 6.*

*All Italy*

## BAKED APPLES WITH HONEY, RAISINS, AND MARSALA
*(Mele al forno)*

   6   large Rome Beauty apples
  ¹/₂  cup raisins
   2   tablespoons pine nuts
      Grated rind of 1 lemon
   6   tablespoons honey
  ¹/₄  cup sweet Marsala wine
  ¹/₂  cup water

Wash and core the apples but do not peel them. Arrange in a shallow baking dish. Spoon some of the raisins, pine nuts, lemon rind, and honey into each apple. Pour a little Marsala over the tops. Pour the water into the bottom of the baking dish. Bake for 1 hour, or until the apples are tender. Baste once or twice during cooking. *Serves 6.*

*Piedmont*

## CHERRIES IN BAROLO WINE
*(Ciliegie in barolo)*

Fruit compotes are served all over Italy. This is a classic Piedmontese compote, cooked in spiced red wine. Plums, pears, apples, and peaches can all be cooked in the same way.

Any good dry red wine may be used instead of Barolo.

1½  **pounds cherries**
¼  **cup honey or sugar**
2  **cups Barolo wine**
½  **cinnamon stick**
2  **strips of orange rind**

Wash and stem the cherries, then remove the pits. Place the cherries in a saucepan with the honey, red wine, cinnamon stick, and orange rind. Bring to a boil and simmer for 10 minutes. Pour into a glass serving dish and chill thoroughly in the refrigerator. *Serves 4 to 6.*

*Sicily*

## PEARS WITH ZABAGLIONE
*(Pere allo zabaglione)*

❦ ❦ ❦

Zabaglione is one of Italy's most famous desserts. It is a delectable frothy cream, made with egg yolks, sugar, and wine, usually Marsala. Sometimes gelatin or whipped cream is added. If this dessert is frozen, it is transformed into a marvelous *semifreddo*, or half-frozen ice cream.

*Fruit compote:*
6  **Anjou pears**
1  **cup water**
2  **to 3 tablespoons honey or sugar**

*Zabaglione*
cream:    2    egg yolks
          3    tablespoons sugar
          1/4  cup sweet Marsala wine
          1/2  cup heavy cream, whipped
          1    teaspoon sugar
          1/2  teaspoon vanilla extract

Peel the pears and cut lengthwise into halves. Remove the cores.
Bring the water and honey to boil in a saucepan and poach the
pears for 5 minutes, or until they are just tender. Place the pears
in individual glass bowls and chill in the refrigerator.

Whisk the egg yolks and sugar together in the top pan of a double
boiler over hot, not boiling, water. Gradually add the Marsala, beating constantly until the mixture starts to thicken. Spoon into a bowl
and chill in the refrigerator. Whip the cream with the sugar and
vanilla and fold into the chilled zabaglione. Spoon over the pears
and serve at once. *Serves 6.*

*Trentino, Alto Adige*

# PEACHES AND CREAM
*(Pesche con la panna)*

This refreshing dessert is the perfect ending to
a filling meal. The original recipe uses all
cream, but I prefer to use half yogurt and half
cream.

          6    freestone peaches
          4    tablespoons kirsch liqueur
          6    teaspoons honey

1½   cups plain yogurt
1½   cups light cream
⅓    cup shelled filberts (or hazelnuts), toasted
     in a 300°F. oven for 30 minutes and
     chopped fine

Dip the peaches into boiling water for 1 minute. Remove the skins. Cut peaches into halves and take out the stones. Slice the peaches and marinate in 3 tablespoons kirsch mixed with 1 teaspoon of the honey for 30 minutes. Spoon peaches into individual glass bowls. Mix the yogurt, cream, remaining honey and remaining kirsch together; pour over the peaches. Top with toasted filberts. Serve at once. *Serves 6.*

*All Italy*

## CREAM CARAMEL
### *(Crema di caramello)*

❦❦❦

½    cup sugar
2    tablespoons water
2¼   cups milk
3    whole eggs plus 2 yolks
⅓    cup honey
1    teaspoon vanilla essence

Place the sugar and water in a small heavy-bottomed saucepan and cook over moderate heat for 4 to 5 minutes, or until the sugar darkens and starts to caramelize. Pour at once into a 1-quart mold or soufflé dish, tilting the dish in all directions until the caramel evenly lines the bottom and a little way up the sides of the mold. Set aside.

Scald the milk. Do not let it boil or the custard will curdle. Remove from the heat and set aside to cool. Beat the whole eggs and egg yolks with the honey until light. Gradually add the warm milk and vanilla extract. Pour through a fine sieve into the prepared mold. Set the mold in a pan of hot water. Place in the lower third of a preheated 350 F. oven. Reduce the temperature to 325 F. and bake for 45 to 50 minutes, or until a knife comes out clean from the center. Let cool to room temperature, then chill for several hours before unmolding. *Serves 4 to 6.*

*Piedmont*

## CHOCOLATE ALMOND BAKED CUSTARD
### *(Bonet)*

A delicious variation of cream caramel. If you prefer, 15 almonds, toasted in a 350°F. oven and finely ground in a blender, may be substituted for the macaroons.

    $^{2}/_{3}$  cup sugar
     2  tablespoons water
     3  cups milk
     6  eggs
    $^{1}/_{4}$  cup cocoa or carob powder
     2  tablespoons rum
    $^{1}/_{4}$  cup crushed macaroons

Place half of the sugar in a small, heavy-bottomed saucepan with 2 tablespoons water. Cook over moderate heat for 4 or 5 minutes, until the sugar starts to caramelize. Pour at once into a 6-cup mold or soufflé dish, tilting the dish in all directions until the caramel evenly lines the bottom and sides of the mold. Set aside.

Scald the milk. Do not let it boil or the custard will curdle. Remove from the heat and set aside to cool. Beat the eggs with remaining sugar until light. Mix the warm milk with the cocoa powder in a blender until smooth, and gradually add to the egg mixture. Stir in the rum and the crushed macaroons. Pour through a fine sieve into the prepared mold. Set the mold in a pan of hot water. Place in the lower third of a preheated 350°F. oven. Reduce the temperature to 325°F. and bake for 40 to 45 minutes, or until a knife comes out clean from the center. Chill for several hours before unmolding. *Serves 6.*

*Campania*

## CHOCOLATE SEMIFREDDO
### *(Semifreddo di cioccolata)*

———— ❦❦❦ ————

*Semifreddo* means "half cold." It has the effect of tasting less cold than ice cream, hence its name.

3½  ounces semi-sweet baking chocolate
4   tablespoons rum
2   cups heavy cream
6   tablespoons confectioners sugar
3   egg whites

Break the chocolate into squares and place in the top of a double-boiler over hot, not boiling, water. Add the rum and stir until the chocolate is melted and the mixture is smooth. Set aside to cool.

In a large mixing bowl, whip the cream with half of the sugar until it holds a shape, but not until it is stiff. In another bowl, beat the egg whites until stiff, then gradually beat in the remaining sugar. Lightly fold the chocolate mixture into the whipped cream, and then fold in the stiffly beaten egg whites. Do not handle any more than is necessary. Pour into a mold and freeze for at least 3 to 4 hours before serving. *Serves 6.*

*Campania*

### ALMOND TORTONI
*(Tortoni di mandorle)*

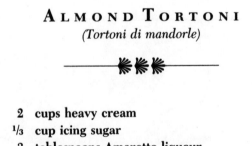

2 cups heavy cream
⅓ cup icing sugar
3 tablespoons Amaretto liqueur
2 egg whites
⅔ cup chopped toasted almonds

Whip the cream until it starts to thicken. Gradually add the sugar, whipping constantly until cream is stiff. Stir in the Amaretto liqueur. Beat the egg whites stiff and lightly fold into the mixture. Spoon into individual paper cups and sprinkle each with almonds. Freeze for 2 to 3 hours or until firm. *Serves 6.*

*C a m p a n i a*

## PEAR SPUMONI
*(Spumoni di pere)*

|   |                              |
|---|------------------------------|
| 6 | pears                        |
| ⅓ | cup honey                    |
| ½ | cup water                    |
| 3 | tablespoons brandy           |
| 1½ | cups heavy cream, whipped   |
| 1 | tablespoon butter            |

Peel, core, and slice the pears. Place in a pan with the honey and water and cook until the pears are soft and all the water has evaporated. Pass the pear mixture through a sieve. Add the brandy and set aside to cool. Add the whipped cream and pour into a buttered charlotte mold. Cover with wax paper and freeze for 3 hours before serving. *Serves 4 to 6.*

# INDEX